ANALYZING CONTROVERSY: AN INTRODUCTORY GUIDE

ABOUT THE AUTHORS

Gary K. Clabaugh is a professor of education and the director of the Graduate Program in Education at La Salle University. He is the author of a regular column, *The Cutting Edge,* in the journal *Educational Horizons* and of the book, *Thunder on the Right: The Protestant Fundamentalists.* He coauthored the text *Understanding Schools* and has written numerous articles in a variety of journals. Using a conflict-resolution approach, he has been training teachers for 26 years as well as consulting for such organizations as the Pennsylvania Department of Education, the Philadelphia Prison System, and the Crown Cork and Seal Corporation, a Fortune 50 company. His research interests are in public policy, extremism, critical thinking, and improving the preparation of educators.

Edward G. Rozycki is assistant professor of education at Widener University. The author of a regular column, *From the Trenches,* in the journal *Educational Horizons,* he also coauthored the text, *Understanding Schools.* He has published extensively in journals in education, social theory, and philosophy. A twenty-five year veteran of the School District of Philadelphia, he spent most of that career in troubled inner-city schools. Motivated by this experience, his long-term interest has been in developing easily teachable methods for conflict analysis and resolution. At Widener University he emphasizes the training of teachers, school administrators, and corporate personnel in critical thinking and conflict analysis. His general research interests are in evaluation theory and its application to day-to-day practice in a variety of fields.

ANALYZING CONTROVERSY

AN INTRODUCTORY GUIDE

GARY K. CLABAUGH
La Salle University

EDWARD G. ROZYCKI
Widener University

Dushkin/McGraw·Hill
A Division of The McGraw·Hill Companies

Book Team

Vice President & Publisher *Jeffrey L. Hahn*
List Manager *David Dean*
Managing Editor *John S. L. Holland*
Production Manager *Brenda S. Filley*
Editor *Dorothy Fink*
Designers *Harry Rinehart, Charles Vitelli*
Typesetting Supervisor *Juliana Arbo*
Proofreaders *Diane Barker, Jan Jamilkowski*
Graphics *Shawn Callahan*

Dushkin/McGraw•Hill

A Division of The McGraw-Hill Companies

Cover design *Charles Vitelli*

Library of Congress Catalog Card Number: 97-65054

ISBN 0-697-34335-9

Printed in the United States of America

10 9 8 7 6 5 4 3 2 1

Preface

We wrote *Analyzing Controversy: An Introductory Guide* because we saw a need for a book that would help people develop a deeper understanding of controversy and how to handle it. We wanted a text that would immediately engage readers in systematic inquiry and discourage them from thoughtlessly taking sides on important issues of the day.

What developed is a handbook that draws together concepts and strategies from a variety of disciplines. Focusing on real-world issues, each short chapter explains how to make a particular distinction, how to apply the results usefully, and how to avoid specific pitfalls in thinking.

Considerable effort was expended to avoid imposing our theoretical biases or requiring students to make important commitments on faith. To that end, each chapter contains a brief statement of what we see as the limitations of the approach.

By demonstrating the practical power of various academic approaches, we hope readers will better appreciate what these traditions have to offer in dealing with controversy.

How to Use This Book

This book can be used in three ways. First, in the conventional manner, front to back, straight through. Chapter 1 provides an overview of the in-depth analysis such a use provides. Secondly, you may concentrate on any of the four areas of emphasis: understanding, fact, value, or metaproblems. Finally, you may employ it as a kind of "field guide," skipping around as interest dictates. Chapters are tabbed, as many field guides are, to better help you locate what you need.

Chapters are deliberately brief so that they can be read in one sitting. All are cross-referenced. Key words are also boldfaced in the text and included in an alphabetical glossary (with page references) at the back of the book. References and seminal materials are contained in the Sources and Influences section that follows the glossary.

There is an optional Test Yourself section at the end of each chapter. This allows you to practice the techniques presented. You may find the questions serve nicely for group discussion. Suggested answers to Test Yourself are located at the back of the book. Since research is central to analyzing controversy, we also have included an appendix in the back of the book to help you do more effective library research. It consists of a guide to basic research, a how-to guide to creating a search strategy, basic facts about periodicals, and some information on searching databases.

CONTENTS

It is better to know some of the questions than all of the answers.

James Thurber (1894–1961)

CHAPTER 1

ANALYZING CONTROVERSY:

AN OVERVIEW

Is affirmative action racism or not? Do women
have a right to an abortion or don't they? Such
controversies often pressure us to make simple
choices: taking one side or the other. This should
not be done hastily. It is too easy to fall into a
conflict rather than to look for points of
reconciliation. Disagreement may rest on
misunderstandings that can be reconciled. People
who appear to be disagreeing may just be focusing
on different aspects of an issue. There are,
however, other disputes that may never be settled.
And it is important to know which is which.

---

*Whenever I face an opponent in debate I
silently pray, "Oh Lord, help him so that
truth may flow from his heart and on his
tongue, and so that if truth is on my side, he
may follow me; and if it be on his side, I may
follow him."*

—al-Shafi'i (767–820)
Founder of Sufi school of law

We live in a storm of disagreement. On TV, in the newspapers, at public meetings, in private bull sessions, contrary opinions clash incessantly:

- Should physicians assist a terminally ill person's suicide?
- Are schools appropriate distribution points for condoms?
- Is homosexuality incompatible with military service?
- Should marijuana be legalized?
- Should immigration be restricted?

What are we to make of the controversy that surrounds us? How much of it involves real disputes? Which arguments can be settled? Whose authority should we accept? Which expert is trustworthy? Does one side make more sense than the other? Of course, everyone has the "right" to an opinion—so we say. But what about developing informed opinion worthy of an educated person? That is what this book is about.

BASIC APPROACHES FOR ANALYZING DISAGREEMENTS

This text contains a range of specific techniques for analyzing controversies. Sometimes, however, overviews are essential. Here are five questions to ask as a way of developing such an overview of a controversy:

3

1. Is the dispute fundamental? State what you think the dispute is. The most fundamental disputes are based on a contradiction. Such contradictions can always be formulated as a "yes-or-no" question.
2. If the dispute were reduced to a "yes-no" question, would the parties take opposite sides?
3. Is the dispute clouded by problems of understanding? If disputants don't share common understandings, they are talking past each other. Their dispute may be simply a matter of words.
4. Do the opponents agree on what the facts are? If not, they are not going to agree on what counts as a solution.
5. Do the disputants agree on what is desirable? If not, the dispute will persist unless and until the disputants agree to settle their differences for the sake of something more important to both of them.

Let's look at these steps individually.

Is the Dispute Fundamental?

A dispute is fundamental to the extent that it is unavoidably based on either-or thinking. Choosing one option undermines the possibility of choosing the other. Many disputes are not fundamental in this sense, because both alternatives can be achieved with compromise and planning.

For example, you may argue with a friend over where to go to eat. You want Italian food; your friend wants Chinese. What makes it an either-or situation? Lack of time, lack of money? Could you do both by going to a food court in a mall? Can you agree to trade off? Could you do Italian for lunch and Chinese for dinner? If you can work it out so that both parties can be satisfied, the dispute need not continue. It is not fundamental.

The following choices, which also generate disputes, are also not fundamental. Can you see how a compromise could be reached so that both options are made available?

a. Do you want the red Corvette or the blue Porsche?
b. Should we visit New York or Paris?
c. Do you want more free time or a larger salary?

Remember, the most fundamental disputes can always be formulated as a question that can be answered by yes or no. They are based on one of the following:

• a physical impossibility

• a logical contradiction

You can't be both in Paris and in New York at noon on June 3, 2010. Since that would be a physical impossibility, such a dispute would be fundamental. A dispute about whether or not Michael Jordan is the tallest player in the NBA is based on a logical contradiction, since he cannot be both the tallest and not the tallest.

.The following questions reflect fundamental disputes. Can you tell whether they are based on physical impossibility or logical contradiction (or both)?

a. Is the Porsche the car you should buy, since you have only enough money for one car?
b. Rather than admitting applicants selectively, should colleges let in anyone with a high school diploma?
c. Should we give mandatory life sentences to three-time offenders no matter what the crime?
d. Should illegal immigrants be deported?

Are the Apparent Parties to the Dispute Really in Disagreement?

The next step in our analysis is extremely important. Find out whether the parties in apparent disagreement would actually take opposite sides when their dispute is reduced to a yes-no question. This may require finding out more about what they have said or written. It could turn out that the persons whose positions you are researching don't really disagree with one another. If so, congratulations! Your analysis is over.

If, however, they seem to be on opposite sides, check to see whether their positions can be reconciled. Remember, a fundamental dispute will rest on a physical or logical impossibility. If reconciliation is possible yet the controversy persists, the dispute may be serving some other purpose. For instance, it may be an expression of a traditional rivalry, a pretext for aggression, or a ploy to create a memorable event. If you decide that any of these is what is going on, your analysis of the dispute is done.

Realize that detailed dispute analyses take much time and research. But, if what you are concerned about is whether you should stay out of it altogether, you can often find out with a short analysis. A short analysis would try to find any of the following problems:

1. Problems of understanding: The disputants misunderstand each other; this makes their dispute unresolvable until these problems are settled.
2. Problems of fact: The disputants do not share common beliefs as to what the facts are or what the authoritative sources of the facts are. Again, until this problem can be resolved, the dispute cannot be resolved.
3. Problems of value: The disputants do not share common values, or, if they do, they have different priorities. This makes their dispute unresolvable.

If you turn up any of these problems and don't have the time for further research to see if they can be resolved, then the wise decision is not to commit yourself to one side or the other if you can avoid it.

 # WATCH OUT FOR THIS!

Expressive Disputes. Some disputes exist merely to attract attention. Such disputes often turn out to be things like expressions of a traditional rivalry, media events, or advertising ploys. Consider the following examples:

- Expression of a traditional rivalry: "Who can give the nation the leadership it needs? The Democratic Party!" "No, the Republican Party!"
- A media event: "On today's show: Should moms make out with their daughters' boyfriends?"
- Advertising ploy (for a breakfast cereal): "Nice and sweet," says his inner child. "Crunchy wheat," counters the outer adult.

The following sections give specifics on each of the problem types you may encounter during your analysis. Other chapters will further develop these dimensions, and the book as a whole will reflect this structure.

Are There Problems of Understanding?

Do not assume that because antagonists use the same words, they are talking about the same things. Opponents may unknowingly assign different meanings to key terms. Consider people arguing about whether the law is too soft on criminals. Focusing on meaning suggests the following questions:

- **What do those debating mean by "the law"?** Does one disputant refer to the criminal code, but the other include the judiciary, the police, or something else?
- **What do the antagonists mean by "soft"?** Does one antagonist assume that "softness" means agreeing to provide prisoners with special diets or weight-lifting facilities? Is the other thinking that it is "soft" to give convicts early parole for good behavior?
- **What do the opponents mean by "criminals"?** Is one talking about convicted felons, but the other also includes persons accused but not convicted?

When disputants do not specifically say what they think terms mean, lack of common agreement is more difficult to detect. We can, however, uncover this kind of disagreement by looking carefully at how each antagonist uses the terms involved in the dispute.

Unless there is mutual agreement on the meaning of key terms, the dispute will probably not be resolved. Why? Because, although unaware of it, the opponents are not even discussing the same issues.

Here are some indicators that problems of understanding are crucial to the dispute:

☑ Different parties to the dispute offer conflicting ways of characterizing the so-called same thing. For example, "The law is too soft; police don't even arrest panhandlers!" "No, the law is too harsh; there is a mandatory 6-month sentence for panhandling!"

☑ Disputants complain that their opponents don't really understand what is at issue.

☑ Disputants use the words "really" or "true" to characterize what they're proposing. For example, "The true law is found in the law books." Or, "Law is really enforcement practices."

☑ The argument remains at the theoretical level; disputants avoid giving practical examples.

☑ Questions of authority of the source of definitions arise. For example, "Do you think the Oxford English Dictionary is appropriate here?"

Problems of understanding are fundamental impediments. If your analysis turns up such problems, you can stop right there. The very existence of the dispute is in question. Without common understanding of the terms, the disputants cannot even be said to be contradicting each other.

On the other hand, if we judge that there is common understanding of the critical terms of the dispute, we can go on to see if the dispute arises from problems of fact.

Is There Factual Agreement?

We can easily imagine one person arguing that the law is too soft on criminals only to have another say, "If you knew the facts, you wouldn't say that." Disputes often involve disagreements about facts.

It is not necessary to know the facts in order to argue. But to argue *intelligently*, it *is* important. To decide whether or not the law is really "soft" on criminals, for instance, would require knowledge of such facts as the average length of sentence imposed upon those convicted of various crimes; conditions in federal, state, and local prisons: the rights guaranteed to inmates in these various prisons; the proportion of sentences actually served; punishment for similar crimes in other societies; and so forth.

Fact-finding takes time and effort. That is one reason why some prefer to proceed without the facts, while others attend only to those that fit their preconceptions.

Here are some indicators of when issues of fact are crucial to a dispute:

☑ Parties to the dispute make conflicting statements about the same thing. For example, "The getaway car was a blue Ford" or "No, it was a blue Buick." .

☑ Parties to the dispute complain that their opponents are misinformed. For example, "He doesn't know what he's talking about."

☑ A secondary dispute develops about the reliability of the source of facts. For example, "You can't trust that almanac; use the Encyclopaedia Britannica!"

☑ Disputants call their opponents "ignorant," "stupid," or "uninformed."

To review: Even though there may be no problems of understanding, disputes can arise from problems of fact. A dispute may remain unresolvable because you cannot settle these problems of fact. Moral disputes, particularly, generate unresolvable controversies because they often rest on questions of authority such as "Who or what is to determine right and wrong?"

Is There Agreement on Values?

Even where there is agreement on the meanings of important terms and also agreement on what the facts are, there may be disagreement on values and their relative priority.

Let's briefly return to those persons disputing "the law is too soft on criminals." Suppose they agree on what key terms like "soft" mean, and suppose they also agree about the average length of sentence for felons convicted of violent crimes, what proportion of these sentences are actually served, conditions in federal, state, and local prisons, and so on. They may still *disagree* on whether or not the law is "too soft on criminals" *if* what they value is different.

If they value retribution, some people might regard the facts about American crime and punishment as evidence of spineless permissiveness. Others, who value rehabilitation, may interpret the same facts as evidence of misguided cruelty that will only produce more vicious criminals.

Here are some possible indicators that issues of value are crucial to the dispute:

☑ The dispute persists even though there does not seem to be a dispute about understanding or facts. (If time permits, these possibilities should be brought up in advance of inquiring into the possibility of value disputes.)

☑ Parties to the dispute complain that their opponents have the wrong attitude. For example, "I don't see why you think good behavior in prison should reduce time served!"

☑ Disputants tend to see their opponents as perverse rather than just misinformed. "Of course, the welfare queens and the tax-and-spenders are against my proposal!"

Controversies rooted in value differences may be resolvable only if the disputants "agree to disagree." This is not as unusual as it sounds. People in many countries disagree as to what the one true religion is, for instance, and yet do not quarrel. Other things are thought to be more important.

ARE THERE METAPROBLEMS?

Sometimes disputes are troubled by what might be called background problems, or metaproblems. Some of the most important of these are:

- logical errors
- consensus issues
- assumptions about the nature of society
- hidden agendas

There are no obvious indicators that we can give you of these metaproblems until we present them in Part IV. Prior to reading chapters 15–18, the best you can do is to keep in mind that arguments may be troubled by problems of logic, consensus, social theory, and, particularly, hidden agendas. Remember that the latter may really keep controversies boiling.

CHAPTER HIGHLIGHTS

Controversies should be critically evaluated before you decide to take sides. There are five preliminary steps to such an evaluation:

- First see if the controversy can be put in yes-no form. Is it fundamental? If so, continue.
- Next, ask whether the disputants agree on common meanings for critical terms. Without such agreement, they are "talking past each other."
- Third, ask whether the opponents agree on what the facts are. At bottom, factual disputes cannot be settled without recognizing a common authority as a source of fact.
- Fourth, ask if those in dispute agree on what is desirable? Disputes about values cannot be settled without one side changing its values or by both sides overlooking the clash of values for the sake of a higher common priority.
- Finally, consider that the argument might be confounded by metaproblems.

Rather than rushing to take sides in an argument, use this process to start to examine what is at issue and for whom it is an issue. Recognize, too, that disputes often involve a combination of the kinds of problems described above.

LIMITATIONS

OF THIS APPROACH

The procedure of this first chapter is basic. Consequently, it tends to oversimplify. As your analytical skill develops, you will recognize that the distinctions between problems of understanding, fact, and value are sometimes fuzzy. But as a beginning, this procedure offers structure and makes controversies accessible to critical evaluation.

PART 1   PROBLEMS OF UNDERSTANDING

Issues of understanding are centrally involved in most controversies. This section examines how. It also explains how deliberately fostered misunderstandings seduce the unwary. Key topics include

- how slogans serve persuasion,
- how reifications cloak urgent issues,
- how definitions aid persuasion,
- how pseudo solutions displace real solutions, and
- how name-calling obscures legitimate concerns.

CHAPTER 2

SLOGANS

Like telephone poles, slogans are everywhere, seldom noticed, and extremely important. Slogans encourage us to foolhardy commitment, bypassing critical evaluation. They also promote apparent agreement while, in fact, undermining practical cooperation. Consequently, understanding how slogans work is essential both for understanding controversy and exercising caution. This chapter spells out how to identify slogans; then it lays out specific techniques for using this knowledge to analyze controversy.

"When I use a word," Humpty Dumpty said in a rather scornful tone, "it means just what I chose it to mean—nothing less, and nothing more."

"The question is," said Alice, "whether you can make words mean so many different things."

"The question is," said Humpty Dumpty, "which is to be master—that's all."

—Lewis Carroll

Slogans are vague statements that typically are used to express positions or goals. They characteristically conceal potential conflict while promoting broad but only shallow consensus. Because of their vagueness, they are easy to agree with; but we often later find that others interpret them in ways we find objectionable.

SLOGANS AND DIVERSITY

The United States is remarkably diverse. That is why Americans, when faced with choices, often disagree. Slogans temporarily forestall these stubborn disagreements. Sufficiently vague to mean different things to different people, slogans are easy to agree with, *provided* we don't ask what they mean for practical purposes.

Consider the slogans used in ceremonies such as weddings. Would bride and groom agree on what "love and honor" means in specific cases? Maybe yes, maybe no. But since these slogans have positive *personal* meaning, they encourage a shallow but vital initial unity of feeling and spirit. After the honeymoon, however, many couples find themselves struggling to reach consensus about what "love" or "honor" means in specific cases. This is an example of how the very vagueness that makes slogans appealing also makes them potential points of conflict.

13

Slogans are not so vague as to be meaningless. On the contrary, slogans are powerful persuaders precisely because they do mean *something*. Crucially, however, what that something is differs dramatically from person to person. Consider a school district that adopts the slogan "Every school a good school!" Everybody agrees that "good" schools are desirable; we often do *not* agree on what good schools should be like. Any experienced principal will tell you that what one person thinks is good, another regards as mediocre, even awful. Why, then, is "Every school a good school!" persuasive? Precisely because its very vagueness *conceals* this disagreement. The first step to analyzing slogans follows.

STEP 1

Identify slogans being used to support positions.

The following are some possible indicators that a statement is a slogan:

☑ The statements are difficult to disagree with without sounding perverse. For example: "Take a bite out of crime!"; "Support our troops!"; "Preserve the environment!"; "Just say 'No!' to drugs!"

☑ Multiple interpretations can be given for key terms. For example: "law" in "The law is too soft on criminals." Also, "peace" in "peace-keeping force" or "peace-loving nations."

☑ The statements are commonly used at large political rallies, ceremonial functions, and the like or are taught in school. For example: the "New Deal," "Contract with America," or "with liberty and justice for all."

☑ The statements are part of a media "sound bite." For example: "The Trial of the Century," "Deficit Reduction," "Liberals," and "Conservatives."

Mottoes

The most obvious slogans are those in **motto** form (a short expression of a guiding principle). For instance, "Every school a good school!" is a motto. Ask, however, "Must every school be equally good in the same way; and whose ideas of good count?" The motto's vagueness helps bypass discussion of these potentially divisive issues.

Consider, "It's time to put government on a diet!" This motto generates broad enthusiasm. Few object to trimming "fat" from government. Enthusiasm diminishes, however, when we have to decide which is fat and which lean. Then we quickly discover that what one person sees as waste, another sees as compassion for the homeless, prudent investment in military preparedness, minimal consideration for the elderly, and so forth.

Mottoes have numerous clever uses in disputes. For example, in organizations, "try harder" mottoes can be used to blame others for the problems that one's own policies create. "Try harder" mottoes are based on the assumption (or pretense) that people could, if only they cared more, do better. Rather than "throwing money at the problem"(another slogan), extra effort is the answer.

Management theorist W. Edwards Deming warns that the very same managers who generate try-harder slogans often require their employees to work with inadequate resources. School officials, for example, may proclaim, "Every school a good school," but teachers may have to toil with inadequate equipment in dilapidated, overcrowded schools that have been destabilized by violence. We can see, then, how such school officials may cover over their failure to provide the resources necessary to accomplish the very end they claim to value. Mottoes lend themselves to this sort of abuse.

Mottoes and Concealed Disagreements

Slogans are handy in disputes because there are advantages for whichever side can get away with being least specific. After all, concealed disagreements are not an immediate problem if all you need to do is get people "on your side." But, when details emerge, people often say, "Wait a minute, I didn't know that was what you were talking about!" By then, however, the slyest sloganeers are already in charge.

STEP 2

Identify mottoes that may conceal problems and serve manipulation.

The following are some indicators that statements are mottoes:

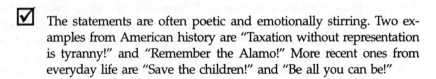 The statements are often poetic and emotionally stirring. Two examples from American history are "Taxation without representation is tyranny!" and "Remember the Alamo!" More recent ones from everyday life are "Save the children!" and "Be all you can be!"

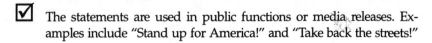 The statements are used in public functions or media releases. Examples include "Stand up for America!" and "Take back the streets!"

We have to be careful not to identify every vague statement as a slogan or motto. Some imprecise statements are simply generalizations or summaries that do not mask important options. Imagine, for example, someone saying "New cars are expensive!" What "expensive" means is unclear. What is clear, however, is that the statement does not obscure **dissensus** (difference of opinion) or preempt important options in the same important way that a slogan like "Every school a good school!" does.

Vague Terms as Slogans

Some slogans are more subtle than mottoes. We can spot them only by looking for vague but important terms used without definition.

Consider "multicultural," an unexplicit but widely used term. There are people who propose so-called multicultural education or who wish to see societies develop into multicultural societies. What multicultural can or should amount to, however, is subject to fundamental disagreement. We can see this by considering the limits of multiculturalism as it relates to the status of women. How much value, for instance, should a multicultural society place on preserving traditions of male domination if those traditions compete with giving women political and occupational equality? Some cultures tolerate wife-beating if it is necessary to preserve the husband's manhood. Should a multicultural society celebrate wife-beating or at least regard it as acceptable?

In some countries, pregnant women commonly have ultrasound testing to determine the sex of the unborn embryos; females are then aborted because they are unwanted. Female infanticide is also widely practiced in rural villages around the world. Should a multicultural society accept these customs along with immigrants from these countries?

How about immigrants from cultures that practice genital mutilation as an initiation into womanhood? Does being multicultural require Medicare officials to fund the surgical removal of the clitoris of pubescent females if their parents desire it? There are cultures where feminist authors are imprisoned, even executed, for hurting the feelings of "the pious." Should American writers be a legitimate target for religiously motivated execution? Is the desire to promote tolerance of difference well served by those who promote multiculturalism? These and similar questions lurk in the vague term "multicultural"; but its ambiguity distracts from their consideration.

Subtle sloganistic words are particularly persuasive because people normally assign meanings they favor without stopping to consider that others probably understand the same term very differently.

STEP 3

Look carefully for vague key terms.

The following are some possible indicators that vague key terms are at issue:

☑ If the term appears in a thesaurus, it is likely open to multiple practical interpretations.

☑ If the term can be used to do a library search on a computer, it is probably open to multiple interpretations.

☑ *You* know what a key term means but don't think others would agree with you.

THE HUMPTY DUMPTY PRINCIPLE: POWER THROUGH SLOGANS

At the beginning of this chapter, we quoted Lewis Carroll: "'When I use a word,' said Humpty Dumpty, 'it means just what I choose it to mean.'" Humpty's assertion points to a specific difficulty with slogans. Those in charge usually get to decide what a slogan means in specific cases. This gives those who use slogans a great deal of arbitrary power.

Imagine a chain of restaurants owned by a very conservative, born-again Christian. (The term "conservative, born-again Christian" is itself sloganistic but at least distinguishes this type of Protestant from mainline Anglicans, Lutherans, Presbyterians, and so forth as well as from Catholics, Jews, Muslims, and others.) Our born-again owner insists that employment contracts include this statement, "I agree to always conduct myself in accordance with Christian principles." This is a slogan. Why? Because there is fundamental disagreement among Christians regarding what, specifically, "Christian" principles amount to, and most people will assign their personal meaning without taking into account that others understand Christian principles very differently.

Suppose, for example, that a religiously devout manager of one of this firm's restaurants is arrested for criminal trespass. Motivated by Christian principles, she has given witness to her faith by breaking into a defense plant and splashing blood on nuclear warheads (such an incident actually happened in the Philadelphia area). Will this devout manager get fired if the restaurant chain's owner decides that she violated his sense of Christian principles? It's a good bet.

The rule is: When it comes to slogans, sooner or later those in power get to be Humpty Dumpty and say, "That means just what I choose it to mean." With slogans, always ask, "Who gets to decide what things mean?"

LIMITATIONS

OF THIS APPROACH   Scholars in some disciplines worry that the emphasis on language developed in this and related chapters tends to shift the focus from controversial issues to controversial statements about issues. The authors disagree. We think that the medium of communication—language—strongly affects what is communicated. We worry that beginners, particularly, will be brought to hasty commitment by unexamined terminology.

WATCH OUT FOR THIS!

Often the question that appears to be at issue isn't really. How can you find out if this is so? One way is to eliminate slogans from the question and replace them with more specific language. Having done this, ask if parties to the dispute would agree on the new formulation. If the answer is no, then the analysis of the dispute question is over. The dispute is really about something else.

CHAPTER HIGHLIGHTS

Analyzing controversies requires an appreciation of the subtleties of language, and slogans are a crucially important aspect of that subtlety. While there are characteristic forms for slogans and mottoes, for instance, it is the way that they function that is crucial. Sloganizing is what people do (and what copywriters are paid to do in advertising agencies and speechwriters are paid to do during political campaigns) to encourage superficial agreement. But this agreement often covers over profound depths of controversy.

Related Chapters   **3** Reification
in This Text   **5** Pseudo Solutions
   7 Presuppositions
   9 Authority
   11 Inquiry Blockers

T E S T   Y O U R S E L F

Although slogans mean *something*, what that something is differs significantly from one person to another. Still, you may find it difficult to imagine more than one interpretation. That demonstrates why slogans are so convincing. It is hard to imagine any other interpretation than our own. This is what causes consensus to dissolve when slogans are interpreted. Different interpretations commit us to different expectations, different claims on resources, and so forth.

As vague as they are, however, slogans cannot be interpreted in just any way. Certain possibilities are ruled out. For example, if somebody says, "We have to get things moving around here," no one will take that to mean, "Let's all go home and go to bed." Knowing what a slogan rules out is as important as knowing that a slogan says little specifically.

Here is a list of sloganistic statements. Make them more specific by creating two different acceptable interpretations. Also create two examples of nonacceptable interpretations. Follow the example.

Slogan	Acceptable versus Unacceptable Interpretations
"Support quality education."	*Acceptable:* 1. Pass the school tax increase.
	Acceptable: 2. Require everyone to take 2 years of algebra (or a foreign language or ...)
	Unacceptable: 1. Let's go shopping.
	Unacceptable: 2. Allow more illiterates to graduate.
"Just say 'No' to drugs."	*Acceptable:* 1.
	Acceptable: 2.
	Unacceptable: 1.
	Unacceptable: 2.
"You can't solve school problems just by throwing money at them."	*Acceptable:* 1.
	Acceptable: 2.
	Unacceptable: 1.
	Unacceptable: 2.
"Reduce government interference in our lives."	*Acceptable:* 1.
	Acceptable: 2.
	Unacceptable: 1.
	Unacceptable: 2.

CHAPTER 3

REIFICATION

Reification is a particularly pernicious form of generalization that lumps people together even when individual differences may be important. To *reify* something means to treat an abstraction, or generalality, as if it were a concrete, even living, thing. If someone suggests that we need to "lift America's spirit," for instance, he or she is reifying "America." Why? Because that person is speaking of America as if it were a gigantic personality with a single spirit to be lifted, rather than a highly diverse union of some 260 million very different individuals.

The propagandist's purpose is to make one set of people forget that certain other sets of people are human.

—Aldous Huxley

Alexander Chase once observed, "All generalizations are false, including this one." This is Chase's clever way of reminding us that generalizations are dangerous. Yet across the centuries otherwise discerning people have foolishly generalized. An example is "Females are weaker and colder in nature, and we must look upon the female character as a sort of natural deficiency." Aristotle said this in one of his less perceptive moments; so, when dissecting controversies, be suspicious of any generalizations.

GENERALIZATION OR REIFICATION?

Generalizations are usually easy to spot. Identify them simply by looking for claims that take the form "All X are Y" or "X's are usually Y," a "softer kind of **generalization**. Here is an example: "Women want mediocre men," Margaret Mead generalizes, "and men are working hard to become as mediocre as possible." Notice it is "women" who allegedly want this and "men" who work hard to meet that desire. But is it true that all, or even most, women want mediocre men?

We test generalizations by checking them against specifics. Find one contrary instance, for example, of a female who is stronger and "warmer in nature" than the average man, or a woman who is not looking for a mediocre man, and the generalizations quoted earlier are shown to be false

21

even though they may have been made by such authorities as Aristotle and Margaret Mead.

One kind of generalization can be often hard to identify, interpret, or test. It is the **reification**. As we've said, to reify something means to treat an abstraction, or a vague general term, as if it were a concrete, even living, thing. Reifications mimic theoretical statements from various disciplines yet lack evidential support. In addition, they are frequently used to demean or demonize entire groups of people.

Let's compare an ordinary generalization with the specific kind of dangerous generalization we are calling reification:

- The Japanese deserved atomic bombing
- Japan deserved atomic bombing

This apparently trivial difference really matters. Did Japanese 3-year-olds deserve it? How about grandmothers? Or Japanese pacifists? The reified formulation makes it far less likely that these questions will be asked. "The Japanese" allows some room for considering "which Japanese?" But "Japan" is so abstract, we can disregard the human dimension. We might agree that the decision to drop the bomb was an attempt to minimize the evil of a terrible war. Perhaps the Japanese militarists of that era deserved it. But we should not let reification distract us from the appalling things that happened to innocent individuals as a result.

We encounter reifications every day. The media, for instance, is filled with them. Here are a few headlines from a major metropolitan newspaper with possible reifications italicized.

- *Drug Company* Did Not Act on AIDS Virus Warning
- *City* and *Union* Extend Strike Deadline
- *Chinese Police* Detain Wife of Political Prisoner
- Clinton Calls on *UN* to Cut Back on Waste

These are story headlines, and, in most cases, in the body of the story, we learn who in the drug company failed to act, which city and union officials extended the strike deadline, and so forth. Sometimes, however, these vital details never emerge. That is when vague terms such as "drug company" are reifications because they function to obscure important questions about responsibility, cost, and benefit.

The following are some indicators that terms are acting as reifications:

☑ Singular nouns, as for example, *America, New York, or The French-man,* are used rather than plural nouns; for example: *Americans, New Yorkers, French citizens.*

☑ These nouns are unmodified by such words or phrases as *all, some, most, 50% of;* for example: *America* rather than *all Americans* or *50% of Americans.*

☑ Individualistic descriptions are used that may not necessarily be true of a whole group; for example: *The Frenchman despises the German.*

REIFICATION IN ACTION

On the commentary page of this same newspaper, for example, there is a column headlined, "UN should clean up its act." The columnist charges that " . . . *the UN's bureaucracy* has long ago forsaken its commitment to Article 100 of the [UN] Charter." (Article 100 forbids UN staffers from seeking or receiving instructions from any government.) He denounces "UN apparatchiks [who] have tried to cover their trail . . ." and charges that "The *UN bureaucracy* . . . inhabits a culture of paranoia, fearful always that a powerful member country or a powerful block of countries is looking over their shoulder." There are over 20,000 UN employees working worldwide at many different jobs, but the reader is encouraged to lump them all together as "apparatchiks" (a derisive term for Soviet-era bureaucrats) "and the UN bureaucracy." Some UN employees may well deserve such labels; but most must surely be worthy and do admirable work. Consider, as an example, those who sacrificed their lives attempting to bring food and medicine to besieged Bosnians. Do they deserve such labels?

Emotionally Loaded Reifications

This columnist's reifications are also emotionally loaded. He decries "UN apparatchiks," not "UN officials." He denounces the "UN bureaucracy," not "UN administrators." Emotionally loaded reifications are extremely common in disputes because they not only obscure details that might weaken the argument but also seduce the reader into thoughtless commitments.

 WATCH OUT FOR THIS!

Personification and Reification—Some people will argue that reification as we have called it is "merely" a matter of style. This stylistic variation is commonly recognized in books of style as **personification,** treating something as if it were a person. But it is all too easy to hide a false generalization behind a "stylistic" facade so that it ends up being tolerated rather than challenged. Reifications can make disparate and unconnected things look as if they belong together or are the result of common intent. They merit special handling.

Reification Leads to Simple-Minded Thinking

Most reifications encourage simple-minded thinking. A candidate for the U.S. presidency, for instance, recently declared in a national debate the need to "lift America's spirit." This proclamation might seem reasonable unless we stop to think about "America's" diversity—something that the reification distracts us from considering. Consider America's remarkable variety just in occupations. The work-force features computer scientists, teachers, railroad engineers, child-care workers, watch repairers, travel agents, motion picture projectionists, job printers, medical assistants, barbers, and on and on, up to a total of more than 100,000 legal occupations—not to mention a host of illegal ones. Think about these peoples' different and potentially competing needs and then ask what could be done to "lift the spirit" of practitioners of all of these occupations. Now add in additional differences in age, gender, ethnicity, race, wealth, sexual preference, religion, and so forth. Isn't it obvious that lifting "America's spirit" is an ambition unlikely of fulfillment? Why, then, does the suggestion seem plausible? Because by reifying all these factors into one word, "America," the candidate obscures not only the diversity characterizing the nation but also the enormously difficult job that he faces should he be elected.

Here is how to apply knowledge of reifications to analyzing disputes.

STEP 1

Distinguish reifications from group names.

It is one thing to refer to a group, say, a baseball team, by its name; it is quite another to reify that team and speak of it as if it were a single individual. For example, you can properly say things like "The Trenton Thunder need a bigger bus." It makes far less sense to say, "The Trenton Thunder lack desire." Yes, in theory, everybody on the Thunder's roster *could be* deficient in the will to win; but it is more likely that, if the charge were true at all, it applies only to particular team members. That is a key problem with reifications. They refer to groups in a way that obscures individual differences within the group. This serves persuasion while it, unfortunately, destroys critical judgment.

Just as it makes sense in some contexts to refer to the name of a baseball team, it also makes sense in other contexts to refer to the names of other groups. Take, for example, political organizations or nations. It often makes perfect sense to refer to the United States of America. It is, after all, a legally recognized member of the community of nations and can declare war, enter into solemn treaties, have formal relations with other nations, and so forth. In the final analysis, however, the United States is *not* some sort of megaperson. Consequently, it is individual Americans, not America, who make the decision to declare war, enter into treaties, and so forth. Reification obscures this fact.

STEP 2

Be watchful for generalizations or reifications that play on prejudice.

Generalization and reification both foster prejudice. Why? Because they can both effectively be used to obscure the humanity of others. The murderous musings of Joseph Goebbels, Hitler's maniacally brilliant Minister of Propaganda, provide a depressing example. Giving us insight into his own tormented reasoning, Goebbels confides in his diary:

> The Jew was the first to introduce the lie into politics as a weapon.... The higher the human being developed intellectually, the more he developed the ability of hiding his innermost thoughts.... The Jew as an absolutely intellectual creature was the first to learn this art. He can therefore be regarded not only as the carrier but as the inventor of the lie among human beings.

Note well that Goebbels is not claiming that *some* Jews are guilty of *inventing the lie*. No, it is *the Jew* who is blameworthy. This generalization, this lumping of all Jews into a single diabolical enemy, is vitally important. It is by this means that Goebbels demonized millions with a single stroke.

We see, then, that prejudicial stereotypes depend heavily on reifications. "The Jew is . . . "; "The Black man never . . . "; "The White man always . . ." Such reifications depersonalize, sometimes with murderous consequences. Thus, Hitler reified "the Jews," treating them as if they were of one mind, one purpose, one identity. Sadly, that made "them" much easier to hate and kill. Once they were reified into sameness, it wasn't a question of murdering six million distinctly different individuals but simply of " . . . defending against the Jew."

STEP 3

Reduce reifications by replacing them first with smaller groups and then, if possible, by replacing them with individuals.

When you spot a reification, first see if you can reduce it to smaller groups with more specific characteristics. For instance, replace "Canada" or "General Motors" with a phrase indicating a smaller group within Canada or General Motors. For example, you could choose *rural homesteaders* in Canada, *retired* Canadians, the *top management* of General Motors, or retired General Motors assembly-line workers. It's even more revealing if you can further reduce the reification to individuals. Consider the statement "Canadians are having second thoughts about NAFTA." Here the implication is that all of Canada thinks with one mind. But one can readily imagine that there are many individual Canadians profiting because of NAFTA.

In *Taking Sides: Clashing Views on Controversial Issues in Race and Ethnicity* (Guilford, CT: Dushkin, 1994, p. 268), Paul Kazim makes the following assertion: "Italy is now a society worried by the implications of its increasing dependency on cheap, illegal, foreign labour." Does this mean that the great majority of Italians, or even a sizable minority of Italians, are so worried? Are doctors from Florence and bricklayers from Pisa equally worried, if worried at all? What about Italians who profit from cheap, illegal, foreign labor? Or even the broader group of consumers who save money because of it? These considerations are obscured by the author's reification.

STEP 4

Apply personal attributes to suspected reifications.

Try applying personal attributes, such as hating chocolate or needing fresh air, to suspected reifications and see if they still make sense. For example, "America is slimming down" could be made more specific with "America has a 32-inch waist." Does that still make sense? If it doesn't, the suspected term, in this case "America," is a full-blown reification. What about "America needs its spirit lifted"? Substitute, "America needs three Prozac antidepressant tablets daily after meals." Clearly, the original statement is a reification.

LIMITATIONS
OF THIS APPROACH

Scholars will differ on what counts as a reification. Some may say that because we, for the sake of beginner accessibility, take a commonsense approach, our approach tends to be reductionistic. In this chapter, we perceive our analysis of reification to be deconstructionist. (When students become more advanced, they will appreciate the subtleties of this argument.)

CHAPTER HIGHLIGHTS

This chapter defines reification and explains how it obscures key issues in disputes. It stresses separating general terms from reifications. General terms can be defined and specified, whereas reifications obscure important individual differences that bear on the controversy.

In later chapters, we will give specifics on how to deal with the kinds of definitional problems reifications generate.

The issue to be settled here is: Is the question in dispute the real focus of the controversy? To find out, consider whether individual differences trouble the reification. What would happen if the names of specific groups or individuals replaced the generalized word?

Related Chapters
in This Text

2 Slogans
4 Definitions
6 Name-Calling
17 The Nature of Society

T E S T   Y O U R S E L F

Consider the following statements and decide whether or not reifications are being used. If so, note in the last column important differences that are being obscured. Follow the example.

Examine for Reification	Y/N	If "Yes," Difference Obscured?
1. Foreign trade helps America.	Yes	One difference obscured is which "America"; or more specifically, which Americans. Also obscured is what type of foreign trade.
2. The Atlanta Braves are in a losing streak.		
3. Germany is threatening Central Europe.		
4. The orchestra played Beethoven's Fifth Symphony.		
5. Generation X lacks ambition.		

CHAPTER 4

DEFINITIONS

Why is it important to understand the role that
definitions play in controversy? Because many
people invest definitions withobjectivity and expect
them to be impartial. Yet, in the heat of dispute,
partisans to a controversy are too easily tempted to
manipulate definitions in the service of persuasion.
At bottom, a dispute over a definition often turns
out surprisingly to be a dispute over a way of life.
In this chapter we explain how all this comes
together to influence controversies.

*Definitions belong to the definer—not to the
defined.*

—Toni Morrison

Philosophers have long worked on constructing
definitions that are universally applicable in setting apart one kind of thing
from all others. But only mathematicians and some scientists have succeeded in creating such definitions by focusing on a narrow spectrum of
experience. Defining the objects and classes of objects of everyday life is
messier. In fact, dictionaries do not pretend to offer such universally applicable definitions. Rather, they rely on the wisdom of the language user to
put limited definitions to intelligent use.

Generally speaking, definitions are tools; and like any tool, they are
constructed for a narrow range of purposes. They cannot be expected to be
useful at all times and in all situations. Any particular hammer cannot be
used for all hammering purposes: imagine a dentist trying to loosen a cap
on a tooth with a sledgehammer!

EXPLICIT AND IMPLICIT DEFINITIONS

We need to distinguish two very different kinds of definitions: explicit and
implicit. *Explicit definitions* are expressed overtly in speech or writing. *Implicit definitions*, in contrast, are formed through the distinctions that people
actually make in practice but don't mark in so many words. As we consider
the importance of **implicit definitions,** remember that we do not learn the

29

greatest part of our vocabulary by being given **explicit definitions**. Rather, we commonly learn the meanings of words *implicitly,* through usage. (The details of this process are the subject of much debate and research.)

Implicit definitions can contradict, even overpower, explicit ones. For example, no generally accepted explicit definition of the term "female" defines it to mean "childish, incompetent, and frivolous." Yet, if a society oppresses women by not permitting them to own property, to vote, or to take the same risks that men do, then the implicit definition of female in that society *is* "childish, incompetent, and frivolous."

Don't underestimate the subtlety of implicit definitions. In referring to African American golf pro Tiger Woods, for instance, a newspaper columnist describes him as "properly mannered," "articulate," and "well-spoken." Had the columnist written about white golf professionals such as Annika Sorenstam or Greg Norman, would he have made similar observations? Such characterizations can be understood to backhandedly define African Americans as generally improperly mannered, inarticulate, and poorly spoken.

There also can be interesting tensions between explicit and implicit definitions. Dog lovers might wonder, for example, if their dogs can ever be people. Does the definition of "person" automatically exclude dogs? *Webster's Tenth Collegiate Dictionary* defines a person as: human, individual. This definition clearly rules dogs out. Nevertheless, to a family that talks to their miniature poodle, Sam, buys special clothing for him, air conditions his doghouse, arranges his burial in a cemetery plot, and so forth, their dog is a person to them; this "personhood" is defined implicitly by the family's treatment of Sam.

Are animals persons? This is the wrong question. The personhood question is not about definitions; it is a reflection of the issue about how animals should be treated and represents a specific point of view. Getting that straight clarifies the nature of the debate; although it does not, in itself, settle it.

DEALING WITH DISPUTES OVER DEFINITIONS

Often, when understanding the meaning of a word is at issue, we hear the following suggestions: "Define your terms," or "For the sake of this discussion, let's define this term in the following way," or "Let's look this up in the dictionary to see what it *really* means." These suggestions may not be helpful. Let's consider the negative side of each of them.

- **"Define your terms."** Just because a person cannot formulate a definition of a term he or she is using does not mean that he/she is confused or wrong. Being able to define things at the drop of a hat is a special skill that is not necessary for clear communication. On the other hand, a quick reply to the demand for a definition is not a necessary indicator that the definition is a good one.

- **"For the sake of this discussion, let's define this term in the following way."** When a group defines a term for the sake of discussion within the group, it is sometimes called "stipulation." It leaves the question open as to whether or not any conclusion that has been drawn can have application outside the immediate group. For example, we could decide to use the word "intuition" to mean "knowledge acquired without conscious effort" and call knowledge gained from hard study "learning." We might then come to the conclusion that, according to the meanings we have stipulated for the terms, *learning never involves intuition.* How sound is our argument? On the face of it, the conclusion seems to say something very important; but would a wider audience be wise to accept it?

- **"Let's look this up in the dictionary to see what it *really* means."** Sometimes a dispute over a definition takes the form of an argument about what a word really means. This is not generally a productive argument, because it can be resolved only by agreeing on the authority used to specify the real or basic meaning. Dictionaries don't tell us what a term really means. Nothing does this. Compilers of dictionaries attempt to use short, alternative phrases to capture what groups of speakers or writers during a particular time in a particular society have apparently intended through their word usage.

Sometimes a dispute can be clarified by defining vague terms. This often means looking them up in a dictionary despite its limitations. Or we could make up a provisional formulation for the sake of moving the discussion along. We should not expect much to come of these maneuvers, however, because if the controversy is important, the definition will be challenged should one party to the dispute feel disadvantaged by it. Indeed, if merely looking up a term settles a dispute, it is probably not a very serious quarrel.

Consider again the pro-life–pro-choice debate about abortion. If we look at an explicit definition in *Webster's Tenth Collegiate Dictionary,* we find "abortion" is "spontaneous expulsion of a human fetus during the first 12 weeks of gestation." It says nothing about murder. But we should expect that pro-life advocates will argue that what is at stake is not how the words are defined in any particular dictionary, but how they *should* be defined in practice—particularly in legal practice. In other words, what looks like a debate about definitions is really a dispute about social mores.

Definitions usually play an important role in controversy only when the terms they define are being used in a new context. Mathematicians and physicists, for example, do not quarrel over the meanings of such words as, "mass," "force," or "position" because they have traditions of usage that have long since settled how these words are to be understood and used. What causes controversy, however, is the attempt to apply a well-defined technical term to an argument that is outside the normal boundaries of research. For example, rather than make a weak and challengeable comparison that "Mary is not as smart as Johnny," someone gains apparent objectivity and authority by saying, "Mary's IQ is lower than Johnny's." However, since "IQ" is a technical term that requires specific testing, if those tests have not been done, the claim is unjustified. But, by putting it in terms of IQ, the claim that Mary is more stupid seems less vulnerable to criticism.

Here are some indicators that definitional issues may be crucial in a controversy:

☑ Disputants offer definitions that markedly depart from standard dictionary interpretations.

☑ Disputants use modifiers like "real," "true," "authentic," or "genuine" when referring to key terms.

☑ Disputants offer definitions "for the sake of clarity," then never again acknowledge that other interpretations are possible.

In dealing with questions of definition, the following steps may help.

STEP 1

Look up the disputed term in a standard English dictionary or in a special technical dictionary.

Although dictionaries, as we have said above, are not unimpeachable, this procedure normally has the virtue of impartiality. The compilers of the dictionary probably did not construct the disputed term with your special controversy in mind. In the case of the standard dictionary, the meanings they give are normally formed out of phrases from old and new traditions of usage in both spoken and written English. Or, the words and phrases come from a special scientific or other technical discipline for use in a subject-specific dictionary.

This procedure has several disadvantages:

1. Contexts of application and conditions for correct usage may not be given (except in a dictionary of usage).
2. The definitions given may be biased by both the time and location of the linguistic practices relied on; for example, "gay" to mean "merry" is the usage of the early twentieth century.

3. Consequently, a generally accepted implicit meaning of a term in dispute may not be recorded in the dictionary; for example "gay" to mean "homosexual."
4. Most importantly, there may be cultural biases built into the dictionary which are the very point of the present controversial usage; for example, "aborigine" to mean "primitive" or "uncivilized"; "culture" to mean "high status activities"; "homosexual" to mean "perverted."

In any case, finding a term in a dictionary of any kind will only settle a controversy *if* the parties to the dispute agree to accept that dictionary as authoritative.

STEP 2

Attempt to make an implicit definition explicit.

This can be a difficult undertaking that may need special practice. Implicit definitions are best articulated with the help of a group of people. Start the process this way:

a. Ask the group to individually write down what they believe are clear examples of what the term means. Call this the *example list*. Do not share these examples yet.
b. Ask the group to individually write down what they believe are clear examples of what the term does *not* mean. Call this the *counterexamples list*.

   For example, suppose we decide to examine the term "violence." Each person should make two lists for comparison:

Examples List: Clearly Violence	Counterexamples List: Clearly Not Violence
Stabbing someone	Smelling flowers
Knocking someone to the ground	Helping someone up
Punching someone	Kissing someone

c. After everyone has examples and counterexamples, ask each person to read his or her examples and counterexamples and poll the group for consensus. Keep a tally.

   Suppose that someone objects to the counterexample "kissing someone" because kissing could be violent if the kiss is unwelcome and forced. The group agrees.
d. Where there is a general disagreement, reformulate the example (or counterexample) so that consensus is reached. For instance, we could alter this example to specifically rule out a forced kiss. If

consensus cannot be reached (that is, there is only 50 percent agreement), put the example (or counterexample) in a list called *borderline* cases.

e. Pick the examples with the highest consensus (75 percent or greater) and see if you can figure out what criteria are implicit in the social practices in which they are employed.

We can see that the clear examples of violence given above involve the use of force. This ties in with the objection to a forced kiss as not really a counterexample.

f. Make sure that the criteria we have found for the example are absent from the counterexamples.

This is a way of checking on your analysis. Since force is common to all the violence examples, it is critical only if it is missing from the counterexamples.

g. Attempt to articulate these criteria as definitions.

Our short exercise indicates that force is a criterion for identifying violence. There may be others.

This procedure has the virtue of actually looking at linguistic usage and the social contexts of application. Significantly, it is a painstaking and time-consuming process. What does that tell us? It shows us that the criteria for determining implicit meanings are subtle, perhaps not shared, and easily overlooked. If it is not practical for you to do such an analysis, at least keep in mind that important words are usually much less precise than they appear. Never assume that any unexamined term, however critical to a controversy, rests on a deep consensus as to its meaning.

STEP 3

When comparing competing definitions, consider whether their authors are trying to persuade us to support a particular social practice.

Disputes about definitions are not usually mere quibbles. More often they are subtle attempts to promote or undermine a social practice. In other words, when someone offers the *definition* of a term, what they often have in mind is a definition that supports *their* particular point of view. Consider again the pro-life–pro-choice controversy over abortion. Pro-life advocates assert that abortion is murder. This is, in effect, a reclassification that defines the term in a way that supports their position.

The question "Is abortion murder?" is a pivotal point in this struggle. By investigating just the "definitions" of the terms "abortion" or "murder," however, we cannot settle this dispute. Why not? Because what is most fundamentally at issue is the question of changing or retaining a social practice.

SOCIAL PRACTICE AND DEFINITIONS

So far as definitions are concerned, if the social practice is changed, dictionaries will be changed. For example, if it is legislated that abortion is murder, dictionaries will eventually reflect this. At this time they don't. No commonly used dictionary defines abortion as murder.

Ask what kind of society would result from following through on the changes implicit in accepting one definition over another. This will often lead to a broader consideration of who benefits and who loses under different social configurations. By examining the broader issues, we may come to recognize that something as trivial as a definition can have a major impact on how we live.

 # WATCH OUT FOR THIS!

Programmatic definitions are special definitions that are cooked up to support a program of action. This common maneuver encourages people to accept the consequent program without thought or criticism. For example, Murray A. Straus, in *Taking Sides: Clashing Views on Controversial Psychological Issues*, Ninth edition (Guilford, CT: Dushkin Publishing Group/Brown & Benchmark, 1996, p. 132), defines physical punishment as "a legally permissible physical attack on children." But is physical punishment really an "attack"? Why not just an "administration of justice"? The word "attack" already prejudices the discussion. Bypassing important considerations, Straus subtly imposes his values by using a programmatic definition.

LIMITATIONS
OF THIS APPROACH

Our concerns in this chapter are with (a) **criteria of judgment** as they bear on controversy and (b) the authority of the sources of such criteria. For the sake of simplicity, several substantial bodies of literature on the nature of definition have been ignored. (What we have called "definitions" here could, in other approaches, be called "characterizations.") An introductory approach to analyzing controversy is not, as we see it, facilitated by introducing subtler technical theories on the nature of definition. We, of course, recommend more advanced study of the important topics mentioned here.

CHAPTER HIGHLIGHTS

Controversy often seems to rest on the definitions of terms. But such definitions depend on the authority of their source. Thus, what seems to be disputes over definitions often turns out to be fundamental disputes over authority.

Importantly, terms may have implicit definitions deriving from the linguistic and social contexts of their use. Implicit definitions of a term can be powerful and can override explicit definitions available for them. What we do is more important than what we say. At bottom, a dispute over definition may turn out to be a dispute over a way of life.

The issue you want to settle is the following: Are terms being defined explicitly or implicitly in a consistent way by both parties to the dispute? If the disputants don't initially agree on the definitions, do you think they could come to a compromise? If the answer is no to both of these questions, the dispute being examined is not the real issue.

Related Chapters in This Text

2 Slogans
3 Reification
6 Name-Calling
10 Operationalizing

T E S T   Y O U R S E L F

Contrast and compare an explicit definition of each of the following terms with a definition implicit in a social practice. Remember, explicit definitions are found in dictionaries or other such texts; implicit definitions may be relative to specific communities and their social practices.

TERM	EXPLICIT DEFINITION	(POSSIBLE) IMPLICIT DEFINITION
criminal	(a person) guilty of a crime (*Webster's Encyclopedic Unabridged Dictionary*)	a person rumored to be engaged in improper activities
fascist		
murder		
obscene		

CHAPTER 5

PSEUDO SOLUTIONS

What are pseudo solutions and why is it important to know about them? **Pseudo solutions** are a phony way of "addressing" problems. They sound convincing, but only because the proposed "solution" cannot fail. Stripped of their rhetorical decorations, pseudo solutions say little more than "Let's solve this problem by doing something that will solve this problem." That's pretty safe advice. Doing something that will solve a problem, by definition, solves it. But what is that "something"? That is what gets left out of the proposal.

Why would anyone offer such useless advice?Because it allows people (think of political debates!) to appear to address crucial issues yet never to stick their necks out. They appear concerned and ready for decisive action yet avoid the risk of proposing something that might either anger people who count or simply fail to work.

*Far too often we follow [others]
blindly—without questioning their
motives—without examining their actions. We
follow blindly because what they say they
want to do sounds right. We follow because
we are afraid that those around us will
misunderstand our questions and put us down.*

—Shirley Chisholm

Wily disputants know the risks of suggesting something that can fail. They also understand that details might anger significant constituencies. They realize that actual solutions usually cost real money. They know that pseudo solutions sound quite convincing to the undiscerning or the impetuous. This last point is the chief reason that pseudo solutions are popular.

PSEUDO AND REAL SOLUTIONS

Some find it hard to believe that persons of consequence would propose pseudo solutions. Believe it. Pseudo solutions sound convincing and appear to address urgent problems. But when disputants gravely tell us that we should, in effect, solve the problem by solving the problem, they are really

- avoiding the possibility of failure,
- evading details, and
- running away from talking about who is going to pay.

Real-solution proposals, on the other hand, require
- the risk of failure,
- saying exactly what is to be done, and, often as not,
- wrestling with issues of cost.

39

STEP 1

Decide if disputants are employing pseudo solutions.

To distinguish pseudo solutions from potentially workable ones, use the "Can it fail?" Rule. This involves asking, Can the solution fail?

- No identifies pseudo solutions.
- Yes identifies real possibilities.

Consider the following problems and paired "solutions." The "a" items are pseudo solutions. The "b" items are real proposals. Can you see why?

PROBLEM	SOLUTION
1. That party is too noisy.	a. Quiet it down.
	b. Call the cops.
2. Kids aren't doing homework.	a. Motivate them.
	b. Assign lunch detentions.
3. Trains are seldom on time.	a. Improve on-time performance.
	b. Purchase more locomotives.
4. Government is wasting money.	a. Improve fiscal efficiency.
	b. Decentralize purchasing.
5. Too many are using illegal drugs.	a. Teach them to say "No!" to drugs.
	b. Spend 10 percent more on drug education.

The "a" solutions cannot fail. Their success is dead certain. Logically, none of these problems could continue if the proposed pseudo solutions were achieved. But, and it's a big "but," pseudo solutions propose nothing more than "Solve this problem by doing something that will solve this problem!" For instance, will the government's money wasting be curtailed if fiscal efficiency is improved? How could it not? But the solution proposes nothing about *how* fiscal efficiency can be enhanced.

The "b" proposals can fail. We might spend 20 percent more on drug education, for example, only to discover that drug abuse continues unabated. We might purchase more locomotives only to find that trains run more erratically. In short, the proposed solutions might turn out to be worthless—even counterproductive.

STEP 2

Decide whether either or both of the disputants are using pseudo solutions for purposes of domination.

Pseudo solutions also help keep people under control. Consider corporate officials who advocate pseudo solutions for very real problems. This burdens employees with missions of unquestionable concern while it allows corporate authorities to evade real commitment. Employees are instructed to "Reduce accidents by improving safety!" and "Increase efficiency by decreasing waste!" But these can't-fail directives may obscure management failures, such as the role of unsafe machinery as a cause of accidents or the absence of equipment necessary to increase efficiency. Pseudo solutions also deny workers any objective standard for judging their efforts. In short, pseudo solutions are a prime way for people in positions of responsibility to pass the buck and bully others.

 # WATCH OUT FOR THIS!

A variation on offering pseudo solutions is to define a problem in terms of a favored solution. As the saying goes, "To a man with only a hammer, every problem looks like a nail." Consider Jan Narvison's argument that the free market can best determine how to deal with environmental problems (Jan Narvison in *Taking Sides: Clashing Views on Controversial Moral Issues*, Fifth edition, Guilford, CT: Dushkin 1996, pp. 66–69). He makes his argument convincing by choosing only to recognize as a problem what the free market can solve. In reviewing controversies, then, look for this maneuver.

Pseudo solutions are particularly effective if offered to people more interested in appearance than in substance. The following is a true story:

An educational psychologist was summoned to a state senate hearing as an expert witness. State special education funds were being wasted when school districts misplaced ordinary youngsters into special education classes. The psychologist was asked to describe what changes had been made to solve this problem. She began by describing the district's new intake process, the tests used, and the assignment procedure. Right in the middle of a sentence, a senator interrupted her and said, "Look, cut the technical jargon and tell us what is being done!" The psychologist thought for a minute, then said, "Appropriate tests are being used in an efficient placement process to remedy the problem!" The senators were satisfied.

Misplacing youngsters in special education classes would be impossible if, as the psychologist claimed, appropriate screening tests were being efficiently used. That is what makes the response so reassuring. After all, it can't fail. Of course, in real life the tests might be inappropriate and inefficiently administered.

Politicians' promises are notoriously hollow. Maybe that is because, when campaigning, they often offer pseudo solutions for real problems.

Here are some key indicators that a pseudo solution is being proposed:

☑ The solution flunks the "Can it fail?" test.

☑ The solution is only a positive restatement of the original problem.

☑ The solution says, in essence, "Solve this problem by solving this problem."

LIMITATIONS

OF THIS APPROACH   Upon initial presentation of the idea of pseudo solutions, students often find it hard to believe that anyone would offer as a solution something that is no more than a clever restatement of the problem. Another limitation is that there may be insufficient consensus on the meaning of a word to employ the "Can it fail?" rule. Still, this approach works more often than not. And, in any case, the burden of showing that the solution is practical rests on its proponents.

CHAPTER HIGHLIGHTS

Controversies often center on solutions to problems. Often these solutions are so much verbiage, although they may initially sound quite convincing. Perhaps the most convincing are what we have called here pseudo solutions. Their plausibility derives from the fact that they simply restate a problem in positive language. Such pseudo solutions can't fail, but neither do they tell us what to do.

Pseudo solutions are predictably popular in disputes. After all, those who use them offer fail-safe advice and evade the details, such as who is going to pay. To determine if a solution-proposal is a pseudo solution, simply ask: "Can it fail?" "Yes" indicates a legitimate proposal that may, or may not, work. "No" indicates a pseudo solution.

When you are analyzing a controversy, you want to find out if disputants are offering pseudo solutions for problems. If so, do you want to consider if they would accept as substitute solutions formulations that could fail? If the answer is no, the disputants may not really be concerned about the problems. Something else may be going on.

Related Chapters in This Text	**2** Slogans
	8 Feelings, Facts, and Logic
	11 Inquiry Blockers

T E S T   Y O U R S E L F

Here is a table similar to the one earlier in this chapter. Test your understanding of pseudo solutions by placing a check mark on each solution-proposal that you think flunks the "Can it fail?" test. The remaining unmarked proposals should, then, be real potential solutions. There is no regular pattern here. Remember, too, that situations that one person may understand to be problematic might be regarded as perfectly acceptable by another.

PROBLEM	SOLUTION
1. The college's core curriculum is insufficiently rigorous.	Make the curriculum more demanding.
2. Too many unmarried teens are having babies.	Provide free condoms and diaphragms.
3. Drug money is corrupting the police.	Legalize recreational drugs.
4. The poor don't have enough to eat.	Ensure adequate nutrition regardless of income.
5. Rich nations are not financially helping poorer nations.	Increase the foreign aid budgets of the 10 most developed countries by 20 percent.
6. The news media has a liberal bias.	Ensure more balanced coverage.
7. American government is dominated by big business.	Increase representation for ordinary Americans.
8. The new minorities are rejecting assimilation.	Make English the official language of the United States.
9. There is systematic racism in the administration of criminal justice.	Hire more minority police, judges, and probation officers.
10. Underclass culture perpetuates poverty among urban minorities.	Use federal funds to build and staff free 24-hour care centers (orphanages) that are carefully designed to inculcate middle-class values.

CHAPTER 6

NAME-CALLING

Name-calling is often used to (a) illegitimately attack a person's argument and (b) dominate that person. How? This chapter identifies two basic mechanisms: the **ad hominem** argument and descriptions that denigrate or **delegitimate** a person. Recognizing that such maneuvers are affecting a controversy is essential to clarifying the real nature of the dispute.

The feeling of inferiority is in you, not in any name. The name merely evokes what is already there. Exorcise the hateful complex and no name can ever make you hang your head.

—W. E. B. Du Bois

Many people would not directly insult those who disagree with them. Such people often pride themselves on either their civility or objectivity. Nonetheless, they often subtly insult their opponents not by focusing on the argument but by questioning their opponents' character or motives.

AD HOMINEM ARGUMENT

Two common mistakes can be made when examining a controversy. The first is to accept a bad argument because it comes from a "good" person—someone we like. The second is to reject a good argument because it comes from a "bad" person—someone we despise. Often people confuse the value of an argument with the reputation of the person making it. This may be done deliberately as a way of attacking a good argument because its presenter has some qualities that are less than esteemed. We can find examples similar to the following in almost any news medium:

    a. "It is a typical liberal ploy to argue that . . ."
    b. "Conservatives, of course, can be expected to say that . . ."
    c. "Mr. Smith, a longtime defender of Mafia clientele, insisted that . . ."

In each of the examples above, the source of the argument is identified for a presumably hostile audience in order to bring the argument itself under suspicion. What is implied by each of these introductory phrases is:

a. Arguments from liberals cannot be trusted.
b. What conservatives have to say is wrong and mean-spirited.
c. Lawyers who defend suspected Mafia members cannot be trusted to tell the truth.

But the arguments of liberals, conservatives, and Mafia lawyers can be evaluated independently of their sources. The source of an argument is important not in determining the argument's validity or soundness but in understanding what else might be going on. It is wisdom, not logic, that requires us to look to the source in order to understand a bigger picture. But this is a second step. The argument comes first.

DELEGITIMIZATION: VALUE JUDGMENTS AS FACTS

Sometimes descriptions dismiss important concerns. For example, if we describe someone as *lazy*, we make a negative value judgment about his or her industriousness. Perhaps *not motivated* is more appropriate. Lazy, in effect, blocks inquiry into a person's reasons for not working. It robs these concerns of their legitimacy. "Delegitimate" is the verb we will use to describe this process.

It is critical to realize how easily we can describe the facts in such a way as to delegitimate or obscure **interests** that we disagree with. (By interests we mean those things people value that provide them personally with reasons for acting or not.)

Consider a situation where someone, let us call him Sam, has not done any work after we have offered to pay him $10 per hour to cut grass. We might say of him, "Sam is lazy." Alternatively, we could say, "Sam isn't motivated to work."

What is the difference? It is that the second statement simply explains, whereas the first explains *and* negatively evaluates. We may well recognize that Sam doesn't yet want to work and nonetheless insist that he *should*.

What we are doing in asserting that Sam is lazy is delegitimating those competing interests that he has that enter into his decision not to work. Of course, we may be right in doing so. He may have *promised* us to cut the grass for $10 per hour, for instance, but then decide that he would rather drink beer and nap. We recall his promise and express our unhappiness with him by calling him lazy, rejecting whatever explanation he might offer. After all, he did promise.

On the other hand, if we failed in advance to mention to Sam certain special conditions that he later discovers, such as poison ivy or several wasp nests hidden in the turf, our characterization of him as lazy is, on our part, not quite honest.

In effect, to call people lazy is to describe them as *not motivated to work when they should be.* But whether they *really* should be, given their concerns and values, is something we may not want to discuss. So we foreclose on such considerations by using the delegitimating term "lazy." (Note that African Americans under conditions of slavery were routinely referred to by their owners as "lazy." Did these owners concern themselves with the slaves' interests?)

Examine the following chart:

Recognizing Interest X	Delegitimating Interest (overly X when he shouldn't be)
insistent, committed	pigheaded
cautious	gutless
single-minded	fanatic
insufficiently motivated	lazy
spontaneous	infantile
assertive	pushy
having reasons different from mine	irrational
considerate, deferent	submissive

Notice that for any **X** term in the column on the left that we use to describe Sam, we can understand each term in the right column to mean *(overly X when he shouldn't be)*. For instance, if we describe Sam as *submissive*, we think he is *overly considerate of someone when he shouldn't be.* Again, we may be right; our judgment may be better than Sam's. But whether it is or not, we foreclose on discussion of the matter by using a delegitimating term.

LINGUISTIC BULLYING AND DOMINATION

Delegitimating interests can be a form of bullying and domination. If I offer you a pittance for laboring under the hot sun and call you lazy if you refuse, you may well challenge my insinuation that you should be grateful for the opportunity.

Delegitimating interests is also a common maneuver of intimidation. For instance, we see it all the time in racial or gender-based domination. Consider how women have been described, often by influential men, as excessively vain, emotional, docile, delicate, sentimental, cunning, weak, or shallow. None of these designations consider the interests of the women so characterized.

Here is an example of delegitimating interests: In *Taking Sides: Clashing Views on Controversial Issues in Mass Media and Society,* Third edition (Guilford, CT, Dushkin, 1995, p. 220), H. Joachim Maitre denounces the alleged liberality of National Public Radio (NPR). He cites as an example NPR's correspondent at the Supreme Court, Nina Totenberg, for her "stubborn effort to prevent Clarence Thomas from being confirmed as a justice of the Court." He might have said "intensive," "tireless," or "persistent" effort. "Stubborn" delegitimates her actions without giving reasons as to why he thinks she was wrong.

In evaluating competing sides of a controversial issue, look for terms that delegitimate interests. *Whose* interests they invalidate can be quite revealing. Let us consider a procedure for dealing with name-calling in both of its forms, ad hominem and delegitimization.

STEP 1

Determine whether ad hominem argument is the stratagem at hand. (If not, go to Step 2.)

   a. If ad hominem argument is the stratagem, separate the argument from its proponent. Evaluate the argument for validity and soundness.
   b. Specify the moral qualities (positive and negative values) attributed to the proponent of the argument.
   c. Consider how these moral qualities may or may not affect the broader import of the argument.

STEP 2

If delegitimization of interest is at issue, do the following:

   a. Replace the delegitimating term with a more value-neutral one; for example, change "Sam is *uncooperative*" to "Sam is *unwilling to follow Jack's instructions.*"
   b. Consider what reasons a person might have for acting in this (more dispassionately characterized) manner; that is, why might Sam be unwilling to follow Jack's instructions?
   c. Determine what reasons a person using the delegitimizing characterization might have for trying to obscure Jack's concerns.

WATCH OUT FOR THIS!

Be aware that people can respond in ways that immediately give them power over you. Consider how the following questions imply that you are at fault:

1. How could any intelligent person agree with you?
2. What did you do that upset Mary?
3. What makes you think that his car is blue?
4. Who are you to say no to me?
5. Why are you always complaining?

STEP 3

Determine if domination is at issue.

a. A delegitimating term says, in effect, that a person is not some way that they *should* be. Determine, if you can, whether the person so judged would agree that he or she should be that way.
b. Determine to what extent the people judged are participants in the judging process. Is that process open and above board?

STEP 4

If domination is the issue, consider whether it is justifiable.

Domination is not necessarily bad. Criminality, for example, is not merely another kind of lifestyle, but one that we have a general interest in dominating and identifying as illegitimate. Determine to what extent the issues of the dispute touch on fundamental concerns about legitimate ways of living.

Some possible indicators of name-calling or delegitimization are the following:

☑ Besides the usual, often socially impolite, words such as "jerk," "moron," "Bozo," watch out for compounds using "ultra-," such as in "ultraconservative," or "radical," such as in "radical fundamentalist."

☑ When single words referring to groups, especially political, religious, or social groups, are offered as though they were explanations, for example, "He does that because he is a liberal," suspect name-calling or attempts at delegitimization.

☑ Almost any negative assessment of a person's behavior can be evaluated to determine if delegitimization is occurring. Use the formula "he/she is too X when he/she shouldn't be" to investigate this.

LIMITATIONS
OF THIS APPROACH

An ad hominem approach can be relevant in assessing the overall worthiness of a position. The brilliant criminal is nonetheless a criminal. Novices, in a strange kind of reverse psychology, may think that ad hominems somehow legitimate the argument because its source is impugned. This view suggests that everyone who is labeled a fool hides a secret wisdom.

Novices also might think the authors are arguing that there are no occasions when delegitimization of someone's concerns should occur. While such delegitimization is done too often for our tastes, we recognize that there are occasions when it is reasonable to do so. Jeffrey Dahmer, for instance, may well have enjoyed murder and cannibalism, but we need not worry too much about dismissing his interests.

CHAPTER HIGHLIGHTS

There are two widely used stratagems for bringing a person's arguments and intentions into disrepute. One is the ad hominem method; the other, the use of delegitimating terms.

- An ad hominem approach confuses an argument with the source of the argument. These are separate matters.
- Delegitimating terms are used to dismiss people's interests in a way that avoids discussing the fairness of doing so.
- Delegitimating terms are also commonly used as support for domination.

Related Chapters　**2** Slogans
in This Text　**11** Inquiry Blockers
　　　　　　　　12 Fact and Value

T E S T   Y O U R S E L F

A. Sort out the following terms into (1) a list that rejects interest and (2) a list that recognizes interest.

immature, spontaneous, playful, frank, cold-blooded, focused, calm, bored, self-controlled, wild, aggressive, assertive, ambitious, striving, persistent, sneaky, unmannered, stubborn, rude.

For example, from the above set of words we would put "immature" in List 1 because it rejects interest. "Spontaneous" would go into List 2 because it recognizes interest.

List 1: Words That Recognize Interest	List 2: Words That Reject Interest

B. If you want to further test your skills, see if you can match terms in List 1 with corresponding terms from List 2. Focus on related qualities in the person but from a rejecting versus an accepting attitude. Use this pattern:
"Sam is (List 1 term). He is (List 2 term) when he shouldn't be."
For example, we can match "immature" in List 1 with "spontaneous" in List 2 because they fit reasonably into the above formula, yielding:
"Sam is immature. He is spontaneous when he shouldn't be."

See if you can fill in five more of these:
1. Sam is _____. He is _____ when he shouldn't be.
2. Sam is _____. He is _____ when he shouldn't be.
3. Sam is _____. He is _____ when he shouldn't be.
4. Sam is _____. He is _____ when he shouldn't be.
5. Sam is _____. He is _____ when he shouldn't be.

CHAPTER 7

PRESUPPOSITIONS

Behind every controversy are agreements. These
agreements are the **presuppositions** that may be
shared by both parties to the controversy. By
concentrating too narrowly on controversies, we
miss the crucial presuppositions that they rest on.
This chapter helps you to identify such
presuppositions.

Put not an embroidered crupper on an ass.

—Proverb

Controversies may rest not on deliberate misinformation but on the incorrect assumption that the fundamental sources of knowledge that we depend on are functioning well. It is this presupposition of their trustworthiness that supports our arguments. Yet photographs, documents, recordings, memories, our very perceptions are fallible. We can, however, make allowances for their unreliability. In what follows we show how this is done.

IT'S NOT JUST WHAT YOU SAY

Imagine Sam saying, "Isn't it interesting how often we see Bill and Sue together." Trying to avoid gossip, you reply, "Look, that's none of our business." By responding this way, you forestall the gossip by denying that it is (or should be) interesting. But you also allow to go unchallenged the deeper claims that

    a. Bill and Sue have, in fact, been seeing each other.
    b. You and Sam have often seen them together.

By focusing too narrowly on a specific statement, we can be distracted from the deeper presuppositions that it rests on. For example, both of the following are important presuppositions to Sam's comment about Bill and Sue:

53

a. The people you and Sam see are actually Bill and Sue.

b. The people you see together have met by design rather than by chance.

A real-life example of a presupposition shared by disputants on either side of a controversy occurs in "Should Marijuana Be Legalized as a Medication" from *Taking Sides: Clashing Views on Controversial Issues on Drugs and Society,* Second edition (Guilford, CT: Dushkin, 1996, pp. 135–143). Professor Lester Grinspoon argues that marijuana has proven beneficial to patients suffering from various medical problems. He feels that the federal government is unjustifiably prohibiting its use. Eric Voth, a medical professional, counters that marijuana has no real medical benefits. Underlying both of their arguments is the presupposition that adults cannot be permitted to treat their own bodies as they choose. A libertarian, who worries about governmental restrictions on personal liberty, would immediately recognize this deep assumption and challenge it. The point here is that controversies rest on presuppositions that may in themselves be challenged.

 WATCH OUT FOR THIS!

An interesting way of manipulating opinion using presuppositions is often found in advertising:

Buy new Road-Kisser tires. Now with no cholesterol!

Can you imagine challenging the claim that Road-Kisser tires now have no cholesterol by asking the manufacturer for an ingredient list! Although it may be perfectly true that Road-Kissers have no cholesterol, the real issues are:

• What does it matter if tires do have cholesterol? They're not for eating.

• Why should their not having cholesterol be a reason for buying them?

Remember, then, that in dealing with a controversial issue, we should attempt to uncover the structures of argument that may be hidden within a dispute. Here is a procedure to follow:

STEP 1

In a dispute, identify evaluative statements, which presuppose facts.

Treat statements as being **evaluative** or **nonevaluative**. Indicators of evaluative statements are that they begin (or end) with such phrases as

☑ It is important to remember that . . .

☑ It is good that . . .

☑ That . . . is not worth considering.

Here are several examples:

a. It is important to remember that Sam is a felon.
b. It is good that taxes have been lowered.
c. That John has been accused of dishonesty is not worth considering.

These evaluative statements presuppose the truth of that which they evaluate. Here are the presuppositions involved in the statements above:

a. Example presupposes that it is true that Sam is a felon.
b. Example presupposes that taxes have been lowered.
c. Example presupposes that John has been accused of dishonesty.

For the purposes of analyzing a dispute, disregard initially the evaluative frameworks in which presuppositions are embedded. (Recognize that the presupposed facts may themselves be wrong and have to be judged on their own merits. Even if we agree on the facts, evaluating them may require additional argument.) Let's look at Step 2.

STEP 2

Go back through the arguments of the disputants. Sort the nonevaluative statements into three kinds: perceptions, reports, or deductions. These three kinds of statements rest on different presuppositions. Controversy may be rooted in any of them.

Most statements that are used as premises in arguments are reports. They may be reports of perceptions, reports of reports, or reports of deductions.

A typical indicator of **perception statements** is

☑ use of the present tense.

Examples are:

a. I *hear* a loud sound. ("I *heard* a loud sound" relies on memory, so is not classifiable as a perception statement.)
b. John is saying nothing.

Perception statements presuppose

- that the sense faculties—sight, hearing, smell, taste, and touch—of the perceiver are functioning normally.
- that the deeply acculturated habits of interpretation of the perceiver are relevant to the situation; that is, that, if the perceiver is a North American, he or she is not trying to describe the religious behavior of a Nahuatl curandero (medicine man), thinking him to be just an ordinary Mexican laborer.
- that the situation in which the perception is made is not too unusual.

If, for example, we know that John (who is now speaking!) is drunk or that the lighting is bad, we might reject John's claim, "I see an old Mexican man, dressed in red, mumbling to himself" as indicating the presence of an old Mexican man, or of red clothes, or of mumbling.

Pure perception statements are rarely found in argument. Rather, reports of them are given as premises. Report statements presuppose the accuracy of a quotation or a citation, that is, they assume that the reporters haven't misheard, misread, or misstated what they have reported on.

Report statements can be of perceptions, other reports, or deductions.

a. I heard a loud sound.
b. John said Sam was sick.
c. I concluded that Sam must have been sick.

Reports also can be citations or quotations from books and other print or television media. Here are some examples:

a. *"The Oxford English Dictionary* defines crime as . . ."
b. The *New York Times* reported that Stevenson died yesterday.
c. John told me he was on his way home.

They also presuppose that the medium of transmittal has been stable and has not been subverted and that personal memory, the word processor, telephone line, computer memory, etc., have not malfunctioned or been tampered with.

Final Caution

There is no reason to assume that, because a person is sincerely offering testimony, we are hearing the truth. Someone may report—with full intention of telling the truth—what he or she has seen or heard. But this does not, in itself, guarantee fact. On the other hand, people who claim that they have seen ghosts, have talked with the Goddess Athena, have been visited by extra-terrestrials, or have cast spells need not be rejected as liars or insulted by being labeled "irrational." What we must look at are the presuppositions that they bring to the claims they make.

This is not to say that truth is relative or that we should indulge any old claim to the truth as true for someone. It is to say, however, that establishing something as fact is a difficult and often tentative endeavor. It is to say that our firmest, most established beliefs might someday be convincingly argued to have been based on false presuppositions. Critical investigation cannot bestow absolute certainty. But to forgo critical investigation for this reason is cowardice.

LIMITATIONS
OF THIS APPROACH

The topic is far more complex than one chapter can fully handle. What we have tried to do here is to provide a starting point for issues that have perplexed scholars for centuries.

CHAPTER HIGHLIGHTS

Controversies may rest not on deliberate misinformation but on presuppositions that our fundamental sources of knowledge are functioning well. Presuppositions are assumptions about the sources of knowledge. Our normal sources of knowledge, that is, our senses, our memory, the reports of trustworthy persons, and authoritative books and databases, can be subject to failure. But the presuppositions of their normal functioning are what support our arguments. Remember, an argument is only as strong as the presuppositions it rests on.

Related Chapters
in This Text

8 Feeling, Facts, and Logic
9 Authority
10 Operationalizing
11 Inquiry Blockers
12 Fact and Value

T E S T   Y O U R S E L F

Consider the following reports. Imagine each reported statement to be false but nonetheless to have been sincerely reported by someone who believed it to be true. What presuppositions might have failed? What makes it possible for them to be false in spite of the conviction of their reporter? Now estimate how probable (low, moderate, high) such a failure is. Use your intuition.

False Statement	Presupposition
1. Mary was seen stealing Jack's pen.	(a) The person seeing the situation (in good light) had his glasses on. (b) What someone saw her take was a pen. (c) She intended to keep it. (d) The pen belonged to Jack.
2. Jack wrote that he could see his long-dead uncle standing right in front of him.	
3. The *Sacramento Bee* reported that Sam had embezzled funds.	
4. Sam says he can feel that his foot is frostbitten.	
5. Experts claim that Coca-Cola improves cerebral functioning.	

PART 2 PROBLEMS OF FACT

Many controversies involve arguments about facts. This section investigates how facts are involved in disputes by

- explaining how one disputant's fact can be another's foolishness,
- examining the relationship between facts and feelings,
- showing how facts depend on consensus and authority,
- exploring the foundations of decision making, and
- describing the function of inquiry blockers.

CHAPTER 8

FEELINGS, FACTS, AND LOGIC

The hotter the controversy the more likely it is to involve the confusion of emotion with evidence and reason. In this chapter, we explain how feelings bear on facts and logic. We also provide ways of detecting and combating appeals to emotion—one of the most powerful means of persuasion.

People who shut their eyes to reality simply invite their own destruction, and anyone who insists on remaining in a state of innocence long after that innocence is dead turns himself into a monster.

—James Baldwin

Feelings vastly enrich our lives. But facts aren't changed because of how we feel about them. As we explain in chapter 12, Fact and Value, facts are dependent on human judgments, and such judgments are necessarily an expression of values. But that is not the same thing as saying that how we feel about things changes facts. It might be understandable, for instance, for a physician to pity a patient whom she thinks may have some dread disease; but it would be unwise, indeed, unhelpful, for the doctor to let that pity influence her diagnosis. She would be even more foolish if she thought her feelings would actually change the nature of the patient's disease. Welcome them or fear them, facts remain facts.

Emotions are similarly irrelevant when it comes to logic. Emotionally appealing arguments may turn out to be illogical garbage, and repellent arguments may prove to be perfectly reasoned. Several thousand years ago, the ancient Greeks, pioneers in the study of reasoning, recognized this truth. Aristotle and other early logicians were well aware that the logic or illogic of an argument must be decided on the merit of reasoning alone. They categorized the mistaken idea that emotion is relevant to logic as the "fallacy of the argument to feelings."

Of course, in considering controversial issues like "Should surrogate motherhood be outlawed?" for example, our feelings about surrogate motherhood are a consideration. But we still should not permit emotion to influence our assessment of

- factual claims bearing on the controversy or
- the logic of any argument that is being utilized.

EMOTIONS AND PERSUASION

However irrelevant they might be when it comes to factual claims or the logic of an argument, feelings still play a particularly crucial role in persuasion. In fact, Aristotle classified emotional appeals (*pathos*) as one of the most effective means of influencing others.

Some appeals to emotion are uncalculated, coming from disputants who are emotionally wrapped up in the issue themselves. But others emanate from practiced publicists or cunning propagandists who play on emotions as skillfully as a virtuoso plays the piano. We should be wary of this. Some classic appeals to emotion that you should watch out for follow.

Appeals to Envy

Envy, we are told, is one of the seven cardinal sins. And it is all too common. A Danish proverb asserts, "If envy were a fever, all the world would be ill." Perhaps this is why appeals to envy are so seductive. Essentially, a disputant appealing to envy will try to manipulate you into accepting an argument because of jealousy of the other person.

☑   Loaded language is a key indicator that an appeal to envy is being made. In analyzing controversies, be alert for **loaded words** or phrases that might be used to trigger and exploit envy.

The chart below contains a sampler of loaded words that appeal to envy. Compare the terms that capitalize on envy in the left column with their more neutral alternatives in the right column. Labeling a self-confident person "conceited" appeals to our envy. Calling a person an elitist or snobbish exploits our envy of the person's degree of refinement.

Loaded Words That Play on Envy	Alternative, More Neutral Words
fat cat	wealthy
privileged	affluent
favored	prosperous
elitist	discriminating
haughty	cultured
snobbish	educated
conceited	self-confident
stuck-up	
pushy	assertive
aggressive	in control
power mad	masterful

Appeals to Fear

Fear as a self-protective response is perfectly reasonable. But this same emotion can also cloud judgment. And, as in the case of envy, fear can be played upon.

☑ Some possible indicators that fear is being appealed to are the use of the left-column terms instead of the right-column terms in the chart below.

Loaded Words Appealing to Fear	Alternative, More Neutral Words
bully	assertive
aggressive	self-confident
sneaky	cautious
underhanded	circumspect
furtive	discreet
surreptitious	watchful
out-of-control	spontaneous
impulsive	freewheeling
rash	instinctive
reckless	carefree

The point is that the same essential trait or behavior can be referred to in a way that plays on our feelings—in this case, fear.

Appeals to Hatred

Hatred is strangely seductive, and zealots of every stripe seem to need a devil. Hitler, for instance, demonized the Jews, and it served Stalin's murderous purposes to incite hatred for "wreckers" (of the revolution) and so-called enemies of the people.

Loaded language is particularly effective in triggering hate. For example, there seems to be a nearly endless supply of nasty words that promote and exploit hatred for particular racial, ethnic, or religious groups. These are all too commonly known, and we omit a chart of examples for the sake of good taste. Bear in mind, however, that there are subtler loaded words that also play on hatred. Here are some code words used to trigger revulsion: welfare queen, bleeding heart, fascist, extremist, international banker, one-worlder, tree-hugger, union buster, puritan, bureaucrat, shyster, and draft dodger. Of course, there are many, many more. We do not intend here to provide an exhaustive list, but simply to remind you that in polite company, appeals to hatred are made in this indirect way.

Appeals to Pride

Pride is another of the so-called seven deadly sins—the one, we are told, that most surely separates a sinner from the grace of God. Often we can spot appeals to pride by looking for characteristic indicator phrases like the following:

☑ Any educated (or substitute intelligent, upstanding, healthy) person knows that . . .

☑ A person with your good background (education, breeding) can't help but see that . . .

☑ You will be proud to know that . . .

An inverse appeal to pride plays on our fear of seeming stupid. Persuasion professionals are well aware of this and cleverly use it to their advantage. To make you feel alone and stupid in your opinions, for instance, they might commission a poll with loaded questions; then release the findings to the press. Essentially they are saying "Look at all the people who agree with us. You must be wrong." Be alert for such maneuvers.

In the final analysis, pride unsupported by fact is merely vanity.

 WATCH OUT FOR THIS!

By putting a subtle twist on the appeal to pride, publicists and propagandists get people to join causes by exploiting the need to feel more important or powerful. Hitler, for instance, announced that he wanted to see once more in the eyes of youth "the gleam of pride and independence of the beast of prey." He told members of his Hitler Youth that they were to be "swift as greyhounds, tough as leather, and hard as Krupp steel." What insecure adolescent boy wouldn't like to imagine himself that way? Watch out for such entreaties. They work all too well—particularly when those targeted feel insecure or have low self-esteem.

Appeals to Moderation

Imagine the following debate: "1 plus 1 equals 2," says Jane. "No!" says Harry, "1 plus 1 equals 3." Max, ever the mediator, pushes for the following middle course, "Why don't we agree for practical purposes that 1 plus 1 equals 2½? We each give a little, we each gain a little." This silly story demonstrates that moderation may not always help you to get the best answer. Still, in subtler disputes, appeals to moderation are emotionally tempting. After all, they appeal to a person's desire to be (or, at least, seem to be) tolerant, reasonable, and accommodating. But lazy tolerance, that is, tolerance that ignores facts or logic, may be merely error.

Appeals to Reciprocity

The most skilled persuaders employ more subtle appeals to emotion, which might be called second-order appeals. Their strategy depends on people's need to return favors or match concessions. A religious cult, for instance, might "give" a flower before asking for a donation. Some indicators of appeals to reciprocity follow:

- ☑ unsolicited "gifts"
- ☑ favors
- ☑ concessions

Behavioral scientists call this disposition to give something in return the **rule of reciprocation**. Be mindful of this highly effective technique. It is a way of inserting the thin edge of the wedge to gain favor.

Appeals to Consistency

The desire to want to be (and look) consistent is the basis for another clever second-order persuasion technique. If you can be convinced to make some minor commitment—something like signing a petition—you are likely to behave in the future in ways that are consistent with that commitment. In other words, once you are induced into minor initial action, momentum takes over. Keep in mind that somebody might be using this maneuver to suck you into a whirlpool of deeper commitments.

A Last Word about Loaded Language

Loaded words figure heavily in appeals to emotion. But keep in mind that the emotional charge of words varies from person to person or group to group. "Conservative," for example, triggers negative feelings in some but positive ones in others. "Liberal" has the same bipolar effect. Words of this type work well as emotional appeals only with audiences of relatively uniform character. This limits their usefulness in a broad-based dispute.

Other words have far more uniform positive or negative connotations. When public officials become "politicians," for instance, it inspires nearly universal distaste. Emotionally broad-based words are the type of terminology most likely encountered in a multipartisan context.

Keep in mind also that contrastive nouns, such as *general* vs. *warlord*, *secret agent* vs. *spy*, *terrorist* vs. *freedom fighter*, or *bribe* vs. *gift* are not the only type of emotionally charged words that disputants use. Contrastive adjectives, such as: *generous* vs. *wasteful* or *rude* vs. *forthright*, and contrastive adverbs, such as: *carefully* vs. *obsessively* or *forcefully* vs. *violently*, serve just as well. In fact, a judicious blend of negatively and positively charged nouns, adjectives, and adverbs is the right recipe for a skillfully prepared emotional appeal.

THE ANALYTIC PROCEDURE

We have established that, in analyzing disputes, a cardinal principle is to remain as emotionally uninvolved as possible. Here is how such objectivity can be better accomplished.

STEP 1

Be ever-mindful of appeals to your emotions.

Texts in persuasion routinely caution against alerting the audience to the awareness that their emotions are being played upon. They warn that people who know this are on their guard. Learn from this. Approach the appraisal of any controversy with caution, keeping in mind that appeals to emotion are probably being made. This reduces the likelihood of your being drawn in by such moves.

STEP 2

Look for specific emotional appeals.

Recall our representative sampler of common emotional appeals along with the listing of indicators. We listed appeals to envy, fear, hatred, pride, and moderation. All are very common. We also described some subtler second-order appeals such as the various appeals to reciprocity. These illustrate that the range of emotions is great and so is the scope of appeals. Anticipate that disputants will appeal to a wide range of emotions—most commonly by means of loaded words.

STEP 3

Try word substitution.

Here is a countermeasure for arguments that appeal to emotions through loaded words. Simply pick out a key paragraph or two, identify the loaded words or phrases, and substitute emotionally neutral language.

Let's apply this technique to a key paragraph from a letter to the editor of the *Philadelphia Inquirer*. It concerns a controversy over controlled deer hunts to reduce the deer population in city parks:

> [E]veryone has witnessed the failures of this approach. Yet the gun-toting problem solvers are now planning to invade the city's parks. Such a movement is being led by a small but loud minority of hunters, supported by self-serving politicians.

We are looking for loaded words or phrases. How about "gun-toting problem solvers," the plan to "invade" city parks, the "loud minority of hunters" and "self-serving politicians"? Now, let's try word substitution. Let's see how this excerpt reads if we replace loaded words or phrases with more neutral language? Here is one possibility:

> [R]esidents have witnessed the failures of this approach. Yet a controlled number of hunters are now planning to hunt deer in the city's parks. Such a policy is being advocated by some hunters, supported by some city officials.

By the way, what are the facts about the "proposed" hunt? A call to the Fairmount Park Commission revealed that park officials had not even conducted the required deer census. Neither had they developed the obligatory deer control plan, applied to the state game commission for necessary permission to conduct a hunt, or held mandated public hearings. A key park official summed up the situation by saying, "Even the long-term prospects of such a hunt are very, very remote. It is certainly not imminent." This illustrates how emotion can distract us from a very necessary concern with facts as well as wasting our time.

LIMITATIONS

OF THIS APPROACH   This chapter will appear to scholars to have a decidedly **positivistic** cast. It does so of necessity because it deals in rough distinctions that do not presuppose commitment to scholarly theories of knowledge.

CHAPTER HIGHLIGHTS

The more controversial the issue, the more likely it is to involve the confusion of emotion with evidence and reason. We caution in this chapter against the confusion of emotion with fact and reason. How people feel about issues is important. But facts and logic can still be distinguished from emotions. The chapter also warns against appeals to emotion, helps identify such appeals and suggests countermeasures.

Related Chapters in This Text

2 Slogans
4 Definitions
5 Pseudo Solutions
6 Name-Calling
12 Fact and Value

T E S T   Y O U R S E L F

The point of this exercise is to see if you can identify and evaluate loaded words. In each of the quotations below, underline loaded words that might appeal to emotion. Then put a plus sign next to those evoking positive emotions and a minus sign next to those arousing negative emotions.

The first statement is done for you. Remember, what counts as a loaded word varies from person to person, depending on values, assumptions, and perspectives.

The democracy(+) which embodies and guarantees our freedom(+) is not powerless(-), passive(-), or blind(-), nor is it in retreat(-). It has no intention of giving way to the savage fantasies(-) of its adversaries. It is not prepared to give advance blessing to its own destruction(-)."

—Pierre Elliott Trudeau

Everything ponderous, vicious, and solemnly clumsy, all long-winded and boring types of style are developed in profuse variety among Germans.

—Friedrich Nietzche

For what are the triumphs of war planned by ambition, executed by violence, and consummated by devastation? The means are the sacrifice of many, the end the bloated aggrandizement of the few.

—Charles Colton

With all their faults, trade unions have done more for humanity than any other organization of men that ever existed. They have done more for decency, for honesty, for education, for the betterment of the race, for the development of character in man, than any other association of men.

—Clarence Darrow

It is the American vice, the democratic disease which expresses its tyranny by reducing everything unique to the level of the herd.

—Henry Miller

CHAPTER 9

AUTHORITY

Disputants may not recognize a common source of authority. And even if they do, they may still disagree on who should interpret it. Such differences are usually fatal to the resolution of a dispute. In fact, people may fight to the death over such disagreements. This chapter explains such difficulties and offers methods for dealing with them.

Authority has every reason to fear the skeptic, for authority can rarely survive in the face of doubt.

—Robert Lindner

Conflicts about authority, that is, about what or who should decide disputes, are fundamental and extremely difficult to settle. History is replete with examples. Consider the centuries of warfare between Islam and Christianity. This was, in part, a bloody struggle over authority—in this case, the Koran versus the Bible. The cold war following World War II provides another example. From the Soviet point of view, it was a struggle to bring the world properly under the authority of Marxist/Leninist doctrine as interpreted by Joseph Stalin and his successors. Another example is the ongoing, prolonged, and bitter dispute over which authority to accept concerning the origin of life. Some, who claim the Bible as the ultimate authority, insist that the Genesis account of creation is literally correct. All life, these fundamentalists assure us, has remained unchanged since God created it some six thousand years ago. People accepting scientific authority on this question assure us that life has gradually evolved over hundreds of millions of years.

This disagreement has raged since Darwin's time (1809–1882). Why is it so persistent? Because each side recognizes a different authority. They share no common authority that can help settle their dispute. Without such agreement, disputes cannot be settled short of an exercise of power. And even then, conflict can persist. In 1925, for instance, fundamentalist Christians mustered enough political power to persuade Tennessee legislators to proclaim unlawful the teaching of anything that denied the divine creation of man as taught in the Bible. Defying both fundamentalism and the law, however, Tennessee biology teacher John T. Scopes taught a unit on evolution. Arrested and tried in the famed Monkey Trial, Scopes was convicted and fined one hundred dollars. On appeal the state supreme court upheld the constitutionality of the law; however, possibly embarrassed by the widespread public ridicule that the trial generated, they let Scopes off on a technicality.

Seventy plus years later, fundamentalists still try to use state power to gain advantage in this struggle. For instance, they are presently trying to outlaw biology tests that do not contain an account of creation based on what they call "creationist science" as a counterweight for evolutionary theory.

SOURCE AUTHORITY

As we use it, the term **source authority** refers to documents that people turn to for fundamental guidance. Documents having source authority include the Bible, the Koran, the Torah, the Constitution of the United States, the writings of philosophers such as Immanuel Kant, Confucius, and Chu Hsi, or the verse of metaphysical poets such as Matthew Arnold, Walt Whitman, or Rainer Maria Rilke—all of whom attempted to define the meaning of existence. Of course, there are many other source authorities and what one person recognizes as such another is certain to regard as foolishness.

Individuals can also have source authority, particularly in the case of cults. Individuals representing such source authority include Adolf Hitler, David Koresh, Jim Jones, and Shoko Asahara. All were leaders of cults of personality and seem to have made up the rules as they went along.

INTERPRETIVE AUTHORITY

No matter how wise or holy, documents can't explain themselves. They require interpretation. And whoever is authorized to explain a source authority, usually individuals in special roles with specific credentials, has enormous power.

Except for the cults just mentioned, an **interpretive authority** is not generally a person as an individual. Rather it is a person *in a role* with specific credentials: Supreme Court justice, pope, rabbi, mullah, philosopher, and so on. Supreme Court justice Sandra Day O'Conner does not pronounce on the Constitution merely because she is Sandra Day O'Conner. It is her judgment *as a legal expert* having performed a constitutional analysis in her role as Supreme Court justice, which leads people to acknowledge her authority on the matter.

Interpretive authority has surprisingly wide boundaries. For example, most people concede authority to individuals to decide what those persons see, hear, and feel. But significantly, in their unique roles, judges, priests, and psychiatrists, for example, are empowered to deny certain individuals even that personal authority over their own perceptions.

Varieties of Authority

Many different source and interpretive authorities are recognized in our pluralistic society; it is rare to find a broad consensus on any of them. Some are found in the following chart. Notice that there is a mix of interpretive and source authorities. Can you correctly categorize them?

Examples of Possible Authority

Jean Dixon, astrologer	Tom Brokaw	Rush Limbaugh
Established practice	One's personal experience	Science
Government publications	Another's experience	Psychic Friends' Network
The Pope	The Koran	The *New York Times*
U.S. laws	The Bible	The *National Enquirer*

These examples of possible authority were chosen so that it would be unlikely that you would acknowledge all of them as valid. Indeed, many people do not agree on which items in the above chart are authoritative. And even where there is agreement, there may be different rankings; for some, religious beliefs may rank above scientific theories, and so forth.

Now that you know what we mean by source and interpretive authority, let's move to the first step in our analysis.

STEP 1

Identify the authorities acceptable to each of the disputing sides. Are they source authorities? Are they interpretive authorities?

Try to answer the following questions; they may throw light on the severity of the disagreement among the disputants:

    a. Do the disputants recognize the same authorities?
    b. Do they prioritize the authorities in the same way?
    c. Is recourse to authority unavoidable?

Remember, the point of asking these questions is to estimate the depth of the disagreement and the probability of its reconciliation.

Here are some indicators that the issue of authority is involved:

    ☑ Disputants disagree on why something should or shouldn't be done.

    ☑ Disputants refer to different authorities to justify why something should or shouldn't be done.

    ☑ Disputants are connected to different authorities by virtue of their occupation or other affiliation.

☞ WATCH OUT FOR THIS!

Don't count on disputants being open about their allegiance to a particular authority, especially if concealment or misrepresentation serves persuasion. Such dishonesty has a long history. For instance, the old Kremlin-dominated Communist Party in the United States routinely set up "front" organizations that were publicly unaffiliated with the party but were secretly under its authority. The domestic John Birch Society used the same tactic, secretly setting up organizations like Support Your Local Police.

CRITERIA OF JUDGMENT

Characteristics that effect our judgment of what something is and where it belongs are **criteria**. In other words, criteria relate to classification and classification determines how we deal with things in everyday life.

Significantly, criteria can be neutral with respect to authority. That is, the same criteria of judgment may be recognized by competing authorities. For instance, being an engineer is possible for people of very different religions. Where the very basis of knowledge rests on the recognition of certain authorities, however, it is not possible to accept those authorities in a way that is neutral. A person cannot be a Roman Catholic atheist, a behaviorist mystic, or a Baptist Buddhist.

People who recognize the same authority may still differ on criteria. Protestant denominationalism provides an example. All Protestants agree that the Bible is the final authority on matters of faith and morals, but Protestants have historically derived different criteria of knowledge from the Bible. Baptists, for example, think that the Bible requires baptism at the age of reason. Episcopalians, on the other hand, discern biblical criteria for the baptism of babies. The Amish hold that the Bible requires total separation from the world for salvation. Lutherans, using the same Bible, find no such criterion. Differences in criteria, all derived from the same source authority, explain why Protestantism has repeatedly split into more and more denominations.

Don't underestimate the importance of setting criteria. The federal government's racial and ethnic categories used for determining the funding of some programs provide an example that was reported in the *Philadelphia Inquirer* (October 14, 1996, p. A3). The *Inquirer*'s Washington bureau reported that the executive branch Office of Management and Budget (OMB), which is responsible for defining the categories used by all levels of government, recently conceded: "There are no clear, unambiguous, objective, generally agreed-upon definitions of the terms race and ethnicity." This confession agrees with the results of the 1990 census in which people were asked to write down their own race or ethnic heritage. People offered a confusing hodgepodge of responses, using 300 ways to describe their race, 600 separate nationalities, and 600 Native American tribal affiliations. Hispanics alone listed 70 places of origin.

Those who listed themselves as "white" included people from the Middle East with darker skin color than many African Americans who listed themselves as "black." Blacks born in South America or the Caribbean did not wish to be labeled African Americans. Hispanics listed themselves as four races: white (from Spain or Portugal), Native American (from Mexico), Asian American (the Philippines), and blacks (Puerto Rico.)

What shall we make of this? First, that selection criteria can be extremely arbitrary; second, that the people who set them wield great power. When OMB officials decided to divide U.S. residents into five groups—chosen from white, black, American Indian or Alaskan Native, Asian or Pacific Islander, or Hispanic—billions of federal dollars and a number of special privileges were riding on it. Disagreements over which criteria to use are not usually mere quibbles over words.

Now let's move on to the next step in our conflict analysis.

STEP 2

Try to identify the criteria used by disputants.

The questions you want to ask are:

   a. On what basis are people or things being classified?
   b. Are there other possibilities?

Remember, if the disagreement involves the classification of things, it is at least a dispute over criteria of judgment. Crucially, disputants might be applying different criteria even if they share the same authority. Keep in mind, too, that there is a way for disputants to reconcile a controversy over criteria. They need only agree on an authority who can settle it for them. So, consider whether the dispute you are analyzing could be resolved in that way.

KNOWLEDGE AND PRACTICAL KNOW-HOW

Consensus on both criteria and authority provides what we might call deep understanding, or (well-founded) knowledge. Knowledge is a term of respect reserved for those beliefs widely shared that rest upon criteria and authorities that are widely reorganized.

Where "why's" are in dispute, that community will still recognize the importance of practical know-how; and practical know-how requires only consensus on criteria. Underlying theories may well be different, but we needn't agree on why practical know-how works. A teacher may know how to get students to learn algebra and may agree with psychologists on the criteria for knowing algebra. But the psychologists may disagree with each other and with the teacher as to why the teacher's method is effective. The practical know-how is not denied; the deep understanding is.

STEP 3

Determine whether the disputants can make do with practical knowledge.

You have learned that practical knowledge does not require recognition of authority beyond the authority of established practice or personal experience, so you will see the point of this question: Do the disputants insist on requiring what they individually see as deep understanding? If both sides so insist, they forgo any hope of reconciliation.

LIMITATIONS

OF THIS APPROACH   The authorities that individuals accept are often unnoticed by them, much less critically evaluated. Because most people take their own commitment to authorities as normal, they tend to think them universal. People pay attention to issues of authority and criteria only when they are confronted with a difference. Unless students are made aware of the authorities they embrace and take special pains to be self-aware, this chapter will be of minimal use.

CHAPTER HIGHLIGHTS

In analyzing a conflict, look to which authorities might be recognized by the disputants to settle the issue. If none can be identified, the conflict is likely to persist. Remember, too, that conflicts can involve source and/or interpretive authority.

Criteria of judgment are also important. They can be brought to the surface by asking what standards are used for classification. We can then see whether the dispute rests on lack of common criteria or on whether those criteria are being met.

Even if the disputants do not agree on an ultimate authority, we should look to see if they might be willing to reconcile their differences for the sake of maintaining a practical relationship.

Related Chapters
in This Text

T E S T   Y O U R S E L F

Consider the following situations with their associated questions. What disputes over criteria might arise? Which authorities might be called on to settle them? Would the choice of authority be controversial?

Example:	Sketch of Answer
Harry kills Sam. To what extent is Harry responsible for his act?	What the criteria are for being "responsible" is likely to be at issue here: Intention, avoidability, and awareness are some criteria for examining Harry's action. Possibly lawyers, psychiatrists, clergy, even Harry himself will be brought in.

In the examples below, sketch out brief answers to the questions.

1. The Argus company is contributing an unacceptable level of waste runoff into the Mississippi river. What criteria of acceptability is relevant here? Who decides? Does anyone dispute this?
2. Art, but not pornography, should be admitted to publicly funded museums. Who decides what pornography is? Why they? Does anyone else cite a different authority here?
3. American industry is not competitive with Japanese industry. What standards are relevant to establish competitiveness? Who sets the standards? Is there a dispute about this?
4. The national monetary inflation level is undesirable. How is this determined? Does everyone agree on this authority?
5. Only religious organizations should be exempted from federal taxes. What counts as a religious organization? Who says so? Are there any disagreements about who can say so?

CHAPTER 10

OPERATIONALIZING

How can controversial claims be tested? Nebulous terms with alternative interpretations often make this difficult. Operationalizing helps us specify what evidence would count for or against such vague formulations.

Untruth being unacceptable to the mind of man, there is no defence left for absurdity but obscurity.

—John Locke

A controversy may appear to rest on a question of fact. Many people argue, for example, that violence on TV increases violent behavior in children. The problem, however, is that the phrases "violence on TV" or "violent behavior" are not sufficiently clear to indicate what evidence would count for or against the claim that violence on TV increases violent behavior in children.

OPERATIONALIZING: WHAT IS IT?

Consider the following:

   a. Watching TV violence increases violence in children.
   b. Aggression promotes further aggression.
   c. Welfare creates dependency.

All of these statements appear to make a factual claim. But it is not obvious what evidence one ought to look for to support or refute each of the statements. **Operationalizing** is a technique by which vague statements can be recast as testable hypotheses.

We operationalize when we take a statement that consists of vague yet critically important terms and develop ways (operations) for interpreting these ambiguous terms more specifically. This specification enables us to look for the appropriate evidence to determine the truth of the original statement. For example, take the statement *aggression promotes further ag-*

79

gression. The vague yet critical term here is *aggression,* and perhaps even *promotes.* Our operations (methods of interpretation and specification) should give us answers to questions like:

1. What is or isn't a case of aggression? (A punch, a nasty word, any physical contact?)
2. How will we determine if aggression has increased, decreased, or remained the same? (By counting instances over time, measuring the force of the blow, or the nastiness of the words?)
3. Does *promotes* mean *causes* or merely *correlates directly with*?

Until some specification is done, the debate over whether aggression promotes further aggression cannot be settled.

Here is another example: Some people claim that *watching TV violence increases violence in children.* In operationalizing the critical terms, we ask:

1. What, exactly, does *watching TV* mean here? Does a child have to pay close attention to it, or would just leaving it on in the background count? What about channel surfing? How do we determine how much TV a child is watching?
2. What counts as violence? Football? Mighty Mouse? A Rambo movie? Documentary footage from a war? The scene of a traffic accident?
3. How are we to determine if kids have become more or less violent? From their play-acting? From their actual fighting? From their arguments or threats?

In its strongest sense, we operationalize when we define terms like "watching TV" or "violence" in ways that can be measured. At the very least we would want to be able to tell whether a child has watched *more* or *less* or the *same amount* of TV on one occasion as compared with another occasion. And we would want to be able to say whether children's behavior on certain other occasions was *more* or *less* or *equally* violent.

ADVANTAGES AND DISADVANTAGES OF OPERATIONALIZING

Operationalizing has both advantages and disadvantages. One advantage is specificity. After operationalization, we should be able to determine whether there is evidence for or against a given **hypothesis**. We can settle the controversy about the issue.

A disadvantage is that operationalizing necessarily involves interpretation and a narrowing down from broad, vague concepts. The result is that we end up with sharper and often less generally agreed-to specifications. People often then disagree on which of several possible specific interpretations best catches the sense of the original vague statement.

For example, in looking at the effects of watching TV violence on violence in children's behavior, we may decide that *violence* should be defined as *engaging in a physically vigorous act intending to harm another person.* But TV's are machines. They do nothing more than sit there and emit varying patterns of light. Obviously, by this specification of the term "violence," there is no such thing as *TV violence.* Consequently, we reject the statement that watching TV violence increases violence in children as nonsense.

This way of settling the issue is not likely to satisfy those concerned by the original formulation: *Watching TV violence increases violence in children.* They would likely complain that we have defined away the problem rather than tackled it. What they mean by *TV violence* is something like "portrayals on television of violent behavior." They might even be more specific; for example, "portrayals on television of persons engaging in a physically vigorous act intending to harm another person."

But what about football? The players are not actors pretending to be violent. They are violent. But they may not intend to harm others. We can see, then, that some people might understand "violence on TV" to include football yet exclude slasher movies because the latter is only acting.

These considerations illustrate how it is possible to arrive at competing operationalizations of the same term. This may provoke disagreement about which is the best operationalization. The greater the specificity, the more likely it is that a complaint will arise that the *term* is too narrowly interpreted. Such disagreements are not settled by further operationalizing but by philosophical, moral, political, or **pragmatic** argument.

 # WATCH OUT FOR THIS!

Some controversies are formulated as disputes about what can or cannot be. For example, "Can sex be addictive?" or "Can all children learn?" These should be reformulated as "Is sex addictive?" or "Do (some kinds of) children learn (something specific)? Otherwise, you cannot find sufficient evidence to prove the negative point. No number of negative examples will disprove the idea that sex can be addictive. No amount of examples of specific children failing to learn disproves the *fact* that children can learn.

Can-questions are not empirical hypotheses. Ten million instances of nonaddictive sex does not disprove the possibility of at least one case of addictive sex.

In the steps given next, we show how to develop an operationalization of a hypothesis.

STEP 1

Identify the important but vague terms to be operationalized.

For example, in the following five hypotheses the important but vague terms are italicized.

Hypothesis 1: Watching *TV violence* increases violence in children.

Hypothesis 2: *Birth order* affects success in life.

Hypothesis 3: *Reward* depresses *free play behavior.*

Hypothesis 4: Use of *corporal punishment* in a family varies directly with *socioeconomic status.*

Hypothesis 5: Higher *reading skill levels* increase *income-earning ability.*

STEP 2

List alternative interpretations for each term. Reformulate the hypothesis in terms of the preferred interpretations.

For example, let us consider the hypothesis that watching TV violence increases violence in children. In the following chart, several interpretations are given for the terms *watching TV* and *violence.*

Watching TV	Violence
a. being in a room where a TV is on	a. vigorous physical action inflicted on another with intent to harm
b. paying rapt attention to what is on the TV	b. vigorous physical action, e.g., roughhousing
c. occasionally glancing at the TV	c. visual representations of vigorous physical actions
d. channel surfing	d. any representation of vigorous physical actions

Note that these different specifications of the terms can combine to produce 16 (4 x 4) different interpretations of the hypothesis that watching TV violence increases violence in children. An example constructed from the chart is this: "The more a child is in a room where a TV is on presenting a visual representation of vigorous physical action, the more the child will herself show such behavior." By mixing different items from the chart, we can construct an alternative hypothesis:

The greater the number of minutes spent by a child channel surfing on a TV with at least one channel depicting vigorous physical action, for example, chopping wood, the greater the number of instances of chopping wood will be committed by the child within 1 hour of that TV viewing.

STEP 3
Identify methods for detecting increases or decreases in the events specified by the important terms.

It will often turn out that there are alternatives to choose among. If the reformulated hypothesis we are dealing with is "The more a child is in a room where a TV is on presenting a visual representation of vigorous physical action, the more the child will herself show such behavior," then we may come up with any of the following measurable interpretations of the phrases "being in a room where a TV is on" and "showing such behavior."

Being in a room where a TV is on	Showing such behavior
a. number of minutes within room	a. number of instances of replicated behavior represented on TV screen
b. number of minutes in room within 20 feet of TV	b. number of instances of infliction of any kind of harm on any person within 1 hour of seeing TV
c. number of minutes not engaged in other absorbing activity in same room as TV	c. number of instances of any physical activity
d. number of minutes in room with only one TV in it.	d. number of instances of actual or pretended violent behavior.

(Note that there are 16 (4 x 4) possible operationalizations of each one of 16 possible revised hypotheses derived from our interpretations of the original hypothesis: Watching TV violence increases violence in children.)

Our original controversial statement, "Watching TV violence increases violence in children" has yielded 256 different testable hypotheses! There is not merely 1 issue in dispute!

There is considerable hard work in sorting these many operationalizations out. Choosing the most reasonable one for research is much less fun and far less glamorous than engaging in public debate over this volatile issue. But without operationalizing, the debate is largely meaningless. This may be why some controversies tend to persist.

STEP 4

Specify what evidence would count against the hypothesis.

Suppose, now, that we construct a possible operationalization from the chart given in Step 3. Let's choose this formulation:

> The greater the number of minutes spent by a child in a room with a TV depicting the physically vigorous infliction of intended harm on people, the greater the number of instances of the infliction of harm committed by the child within 1 hour of that TV viewing.

Any of the following test results could reasonably be taken as disconfirming the hypothesis:

1. Number of minutes in TV room increases, but commission of violent acts does not.
2. Number of minutes in TV room increases, but commission of violent acts goes down.
3. Number of minutes in TV room stays the same, but commission of violent acts goes down.

To generalize: you *must* be able to say what experimental results, if they occur, *would count against* your operationalized interpretation of the original hypotheses.

LIMITATIONS

OF THIS APPROACH   The procedure demonstrated in this chapter is common in many of the sciences. To the novice it may appear complex. It is. However, its usefulness in reducing sloganeering and actually developing testable hypotheses argues for its inclusion.

CHAPTER HIGHLIGHTS

This chapter showed how controversial claims can be made more specific so that they can be tested. A controversy may arise because a potentially factual dispute is couched in vague terms with alternate interpretations. Through operationalizing we can specify what evidence would count for or against some interpretation of the vaguer formulation. Operationalization involves

1. a possible controversial narrowing of the original hypothesis,
2. a recasting of the important terms into countable categories, and

3. the formulation of what evidence would bear on the rejection of the hypothesis.

Operationalization is not always successful but should be attempted whenever possible. At the very least it expands our sense of the alternative interpretations that may contribute to a controversy.

Related Chapters
in This Text

1 Analyzing Controversy
2 Slogans
3 Reification
4 Definitions
16 The Nature of Consensus

T E S T   Y O U R S E L F

Try to operationalize the statement that "gender differences are rooted in the brain." (See *Taking Sides: Clashing Views on Controversial Issues in Human Sexuality.* Fourth edition. Guilford, CT: Dushkin, 1994, pp. 2–22.) Follow the steps given in this chapter. Determine which of the statements below are reasonable operationalizations of the original. Which of them, if true, count against the original statement?

a. Brains develop differently in male and female fetuses.
b. Brain differences between men and women help explain differences in occupation.
c. Females will not generally become engineers.
d. Boys can throw better than girls.
e. The wearing of high heels is determined by left-lobe functioning.

CHAPTER 11

INQUIRY BLOCKERS

Authorities of all kinds defend their decisions by
dodging questions. Using **inquiry blockers** they
short-circuit legitimate concerns. Such inquiry
blockers often seem to be plausible answers in and
of themselves, but appeals to such things as
"human nature," "mystery," "intuition," or
"common sense" foreclose discussion before it has
even begun. This chapter examines a variety of
inquiry blockers to help you more readily detect them.

There ain't no answer. There ain't going to be any answer. There never has been an answer. That's the answer.

—Gertrude Stein

Questioning stops naturally in two circumstances. The first is when mutually recognized interpretive authority is cited. "Why is that? Because so-and-so (whom we defer to) indicates that it is so." Why should we take the house plants indoors? Because the weatherperson says there will be a frost tonight. End of question. Go on to something else.

The second occasion that questioning stops naturally is when something must be done. We then proceed, often with misgivings and unanswered questions, to take action on the basis of what are only tentative conclusions. For example, we might find a child choking and, because it is an emergency, administer the Heimlich maneuver even though we are not exactly sure of what is wrong. In many disputes, however, questioning is blocked by pseudo answers. These are answers that appear to inform but that actually cloud reason.

SIMPLE INQUIRY BLOCKERS

Consider the following questions and answers:

Question	Inquiry blocker
1. Why are so many people aggressive?	1. It's just human nature.
2. Will we ever understand the universe?	2. No. That will always remain a mystery.
3. Why do you say he's dishonest?	3. I just *know* it, that's all.
4. How do you know that is right?	4. It's a matter of intuition.
5. How do you know that?	5. It's obvious to anyone who: a. isn't an idiot, pervert, or criminal! b. has any common sense!
6. How do you know that?	6. It's a matter of faith!
7. Why do you think he's dangerous?	7. I feel he's going to hurt somebody.

Many of these answers fall into more than one problem area. All of them end discussion.

Let's examine each question and its answer.

1. Q: Why are so many people aggressive?
   A: It's just human nature.

The answer that it is just human nature introduces terms that are obscure. Does anyone know what "human nature" is? Some claim to, but there is no consensus on this. Is human nature supposed to be something common to all humans? Is it basically unchangeable? Most of us have met only a minutely small fraction of the 5 or so billion people on this planet. Even mass studies of populations seldom collect even sparse information on more than a few million. Centuries of historical study have focused on only a small number of the many humans who have lived. Indeed, the great bulk of the human story predates history. So who can reasonably speculate about what human nature is?

2. Q: Will we ever understand the universe?
   A: No. That will always remain a mystery

No, because—says the respondent—the universe will always remain a mystery. But what is a "mystery"? If people call something a "mystery," they might merely mean that they personally don't know—or know anybody who does know—the answer. We have the right to ask, "How do you know it's a mystery? Are you saying that no one can ever know? How would you know?" If they insist on this *mystery*, it may indicate that they feel their argument is vulnerable; our questioning is "drilling close to the nerve."

   3. Q: Why do you say he's dishonest?
       A: I just *know* it, that's all.

This is not an answer so much as a refusal to give an answer. We ask for reasons; our respondent refuses to give them to us. We might expect a child to be unable to articulate a reason for its belief, but when an adult can't, or won't, we had better be very reluctant to accept it on face value.

   4. Q: How do you know that is right?
       A: It's a matter of intuition.

The person using this inquiry stopper seems to claim a special power that assures him that he cannot be mistaken. Some people trust what they call intuition; and they may honestly not know how they have come to a conclusion. Perhaps we can continue the inquiry and help them to realize the steps that led them to believe what they do. But it is risky to rely on anyone's claim to intuition, especially if the issue at stake is a serious one.

   5. Q: How do you know that?
       A: It's obvious to anyone who isn't an idiot, pervert, or criminal or who has any common sense!

Question 5 is blocked by a response that is an insult. It's obvious to anyone who isn't an idiot, pervert, or criminal or who has any common sense. This blocks inquiry but is clearly not an answer. It is a refusal to answer. It is, happily, nowhere as subtle as the examples we have seen earlier, and, therefore, easier to spot.

   6. Q: How do you know that?
       A: It's a matter of faith!

There are many faiths in the world and one person's faith is another's foolishness. That is why an appeal to faith works only within a community of believers. In general, it puts an end to questioning without providing an answer that would be satisfactory to anyone but a believer.

   7. Q: Why do you think he's dangerous?
       A: I feel he's going to hurt somebody.

To answer this question on the basis of feeling is not to answer it at all. "I feel he is going to hurt someone" just brings up the question of whether we or anyone else—or even you yourself —should trust your feelings. Why should they be any more reliable than any other passing whim, suspicion, or worry? If faith is not a guarantee of fact, feeling is even less so.

In general those who offer inquiry stoppers as answers defend their responses by insisting that there is nothing further to explain or that can be explained. It is far from clear how the respondents have come to know what they claim to know. How does anyone know that something *can't* be explained? The best we can say is that we don't now know how to explain something and that we don't presently know of anyone who can explain it. Going beyond that is presumptuous.

All of these considerations lead us to some simple steps in dealing with potential inquiry blockers.

STEP 1

Identify an inquiry blocker using these indicators:

☑ Answers that contain terms that are more obscure than those in the original question, for example, human nature, mystery, conviction, intuition, "natural" goal

☑ An answerer who uses such a term insists that there is nothing further that can be explained.

For example, J. Gay-Williams (*Taking Sides: Clashing Views on Controversial Moral Issues.* Fifth edition, Guilford, CT: Dushkin, 1996., pp. 290–300) points out that many bodily reflexes and responses have the effect of prolonging life. Euthanasia is immoral, he concludes, because it "does violence to (the body's) natural goal of survival." He does not explain what a "natural goal" is. Rather, he confuses natural functions with goals, as if rocks roll downhill because they have the goal of getting to the bottom. Thus, when Gay-Williams makes his point as an argument from "nature," it has the effect of stopping inquiry.

 WATCH OUT FOR THIS!

Note that deep convictions or intuitions do not guarantee fact. "It is my deepest conviction that he is dishonest" is not the same as "He is dishonest." Nor does "My intuition tells me he is dishonest" prove that he is dishonest.

STEP 2

To ward off an inquiry blocker, ask "How do you know that?"

You may get a perplexed response at this point, maybe an insistent "It's just obvious!" But if your respondents go on to offer further explanation, you have succeeded in averting the blockage. If they start to break off conversation, you have a choice to make. Do you want to maintain dialogue? If so, try the following:

STEP 3

Use the same inquiry blocker to justify a contrary statement. Is there any reason to choose one over the other?

For example, if a person claims that "It's human nature to take risks," offer "Perhaps it is human nature to avoid risks" and see if you can pursue discussion on what would count as evidence in favor of one claim or the other.

That something is a point of faith does not establish it as a fact. If you ask Christians whether their one god is three persons, most will say this is true and that they know this as a point of faith in the teachings of their church. If you then consider that according to the Koran god is one, and that this is another point of faith, believed by millions of Muslims, the issue seems to be far from settled between Christians and Muslims. Some disputes over belief cannot be resolved because they cannot be clarified by facts and must remain points of faith. When that happens, tolerance of different points of faith becomes important.

LIMITATIONS
OF THIS APPROACH

Not every answer that brings inquiry to an end is an inquiry blocker. There are legitimate answers to many questions. Even, occasionally, mysterious ones. As we are careful and develop experience, this distinction will become easier to make.

CHAPTER HIGHLIGHTS

Inquiry ends naturally by finding a commonly recognized authority or by adopting a tentative conclusion for the sake of action. But inquiry blockers are often used to end investigation prematurely.

Inquiry blockers contain terms that are in and of themselves obscure, for example, human nature, mystery, conviction, and intuition. Those who offer them as answers will defend them by insisting that there is nothing further that can or will be explained. There may well be.

Inquiry blocking can be countered by insisting that those employing blockers explain how they know that explanation is at an end. Written arguments that contain inquiry blockers that offer no justification for the blocking indicate a major weakness in the argument.

Related Chapters
in This Text

4 Definitions
5 Pseudo Solutions
7 Presuppositions
8 Feelings, Facts, and Logic
18 Why Controversies Persist

T E S T   Y O U R S E L F

Reformulate the inquiry-blocking statements given below as questions that pursue further inquiry, for example:

"It is clear that he doesn't know what he is talking about" becomes
"Does he know what he is talking about?"

1. It's natural for him to expect more than he deserves.
2. Not you, nor I, nor anyone knows why oats, peas, beans, or barley grows.
3. I just know he's a murderer!
4. A little bird told me that she's in love with him.
5. Sure, Joe's selfish; that's just human nature.

PART 3 PROBLEMS OF VALUE

In a diverse society, such as the United States, people disagree on what is right or wrong, good or bad, important or unimportant, useful or useless, beautiful or ugly. And this clash of values is of central importance in many controversies.

Sometimes these value disagreements collide head-on. But they can also creep into disputes where they work their mischief more subtly. In either case, however, problems of value are important.

This section examines

- how facts differ from yet are influenced by values,
- how values figure into costs and benefits, and
- how values relate to the assigning of credit or blame.

CHAPTER 12

Fact and Value

Facts and values are inevitably involved in every dispute. But two competing assumptions about them hamper our understanding of controversies. The first belief is that "real" facts are entirely independent of human judgments, that "absolute objectivity" can always be appealed to in order to settle any controversy. Since "real" facts are there to be known, persistent controversy must rest on ignorance. The rival assumption is that all standards of judgment inevitably rest on individual values; that we can't agree on common standards unless we become, in effect, the same individual. And since we can't all be the same individual, the only ways of settling a controversy are through either domination or resignation.

Do not be amazed by the true dragon.

—Dogen

Many people think of facts as some kind of little stones, "hard data" as they are sometimes called. They think there is no question that such facts are "really there." All they have to do is find them and pick them up. "Knowledge of fact" from this point of view possesses a "hard objectivity." Facts are what's real.

This image of facts does not help us understand the variety and depth of controversy that exist in the world. When a controversy arises, each side takes itself to be dealing in hard, stony fact and rushes to the conclusion that its opponent can't tell a stone from a shadow. But can *argument* settle such disagreements?

CHAPTER 12

THE DEPENDENCE OF FACT ON AUTHORITY

In order to analyze controversy, we must realize that what people understand to be fact depends on the conditions of authority, **community,** and **evidential usage** that are present at the time of the disagreement.

This is to say that what counts as a fact will depend on

• which **communities of judgment** are involved in the dispute,
• what authorities they recognize as appropriate, and
• what they are willing to admit as evidence.

This characterization of fact opens up a way to understand persistent disputes and to recognize how deeply rooted they may be.

Fact and Authority

Some religious communities take sickness to be a visitation from an evil spirit or the withdrawal of God's grace. Aren't they mistaken? Aren't those who understand sickness to be the result of bacteria or viruses *really* in possession of the facts? Don't they *prove* their superior grasp of fact by curing the illness with a serum?

An authority from one of these religious communities might offer a different interpretation. The serum is a "tool of Grace" by which the evil spirit is driven out. And those bacteria—which they can see under a microscope just as well as we can—are a physical manifestation of the demon causing the illness.

It is important to realize that so long as it is important to this religious community to see changes in the world as the interaction of spirits, and so long as they can translate, without too much practical disadvantage, what we say in our language into theirs, there can be no argument that will definitively demonstrate that our "scientific" conception of fact is better than theirs.

But, if they should begin to die off suddenly and unexplainedly, won't that clinch our argument? Won't the desire for pure survival shift their conceptions of authority, and consequently of fact? Maybe, but only if they value physical survival above maintaining the belief system of their community.

The characterization of something as fact depends on the authorities that are recognized in a community. This helps us understand a common controversy in America. Many think that the evidential rules used in criminal cases are an affront to common sense. Consider a courtroom in which a judge does not admit as trial evidence a murder weapon seized by police in an illegal search. To the "common sense" community, untrained in the practice of law, the weapon is a hard fact. In the courtroom, however, for the purposes of this particular trial, the weapon does not exist. This again shows how authority can determine the nature of fact in a particular context.

IS SENSE EXPERIENCE THE BASIC AUTHORITY?

It makes many of us uncomfortable to think of fact as relative to a specific community and its authorities. This seems to be too **relativistic**. After all, there are many kinds of authorities recognized across diverse communities. And trying to define just what a community is, is problematic. Can't we rely on plain old sense experience: what we see, feel, hear, smell, and taste?

No, but . . . cross your middle finger over your index finger (either hand will do). Close your eyes. Touch the tip of your nose. You will feel two nose tips. But you don't have two noses. When you see pools of water on a hot summer highway, you know what you see isn't real. And the room that feels warm to a person coming in from the cold can feel chilly to a person who has been sitting in it quietly.

What we rely on to judge some of our perceptions as illusory is a kind of theory. The exact nature of this theory is still a controversial issue among philosophers and scientists. What is clear is that illusions do not come labeled as such: it requires an exercise in judgment to distinguish them from factual perceptions.

The possibility of illusion or misperception shows one thing. Perception alone does not provide us with the hard facts we might hope to use to convert nonscientific thinkers to our scientific point of view. They might convert as they try to reconcile their beliefs to the actual life they must live, but arguments alone can't do that. Arguments don't work that way because the authorities that scientists recognize and the authorities that nonscientists recognize may not, indeed probably will not, be the same.

In trying to understand the roots of persistent controversy, examine the context of the dispute in this way:

STEP 1

Determine if the disputants consider themselves members of the same general community.

Do they believe that they share common understandings? If not broadly, do they at least concede that their opponents possess a subjective good will? That is, will they allow that even if wrong, their opponents have made an honest mistake? If not, they will tend to delegitimize or demonize each other and argument then becomes useless.

STEP 2

Determine if the disputants recognize the same authorities as appropriate sources of fact.

Even if no common authority can be found for deep agreement, can the parties to the dispute agree to live together? Or are they planning to convert or even exterminate the opposition?

STEP 3

Determine what the parties to the dispute would count as evidence against their own positions. Would the opposite sides accept such evidence?

If the answer is yes, then there is hope for reconciliation. If the answer is no, there is no specific point to argument (but see chapter 18).

These criteria are harder to use than may be apparent at first glance. We each belong to many communities. Our membership in a particular community is often determined by the authorities we are willing to recognize as well as the interests that we share. Communities themselves may be conceived of as broader or narrower depending on the issues under dispute. Americans tend to agree on general issues in spite of disagreement on specific ones, for example, agreement on the right to vote but disagreement on the right to choose an abortion.

Despite the problems in using it, this step focuses our attention on what might be some important sources of persistent controversy.

DOES EVALUATION IMPLY COMMITMENT?

If someone says, "This is a very fine gun," does it mean she *likes* the gun? Couldn't a pacifist know and apply the standards necessary to distinguish between a well-made weapon and a poorly made one? Similarly, police officers must certainly enforce laws that they do not agree with. Their evaluation is personal; their commitment is to their job.

It is a very common mistake to think that because a person is in a position to apply standards, that person is in favor of those standards. People who confuse this issue are likely to confuse as well the difference between criticism and dislike, as though liking something made one incapable of seeing its disadvantages.

These are simple misconceptions yet so very common as to merit special attention. Most anyone could understand it if someone said:

a. This isn't very good coffee, but I like it.
b. He's a good ball player, but I hate his guts.
c. I find the prime cuts of meat too fatty for my taste.
d. The candidate is unappealing, but I'll vote for him.
e. The best hunting is found in Canada. But, personally, I detest hunting.

A simple procedure avoids confusing evaluation (facts and values) with commitment when analyzing disputes. When disputants give an evaluation, consider whether:

1. They are merely indicating how they "feel" or
2. They are using some standard to support their evaluation.

Many people hedge their judgments by beginning with such indicators as

☑ "I feel that . . ."

☑ "In my opinion . . ."

☑ "For me . . ."

☑ "As far as I am concerned . . ."

so as not to offend their listener, should he or she disagree. This maneuver also dodges the question of standards. But if it is important, we can push the question of standards, asking the evaluator whether or not he or she agrees with the standards as they are normally used.

☞ WATCH OUT FOR THIS!

Facts may importantly depend on human values, but that does not make them arbitrary. Nor does it mean that we can escape criticism by merely pleading ignorance. Don't let the notion that everyone is entitled to an opinion lead you into a pernicious relativism where facts become simply a matter of preference.

LIMITATIONS

OF THIS APPROACH   Even though the approach of this book is positivistic, we recognize the subtle relationship between facts and values. This tension mirrors ongoing disputes in the academic world at large. The reader is warned not to suppose that we advocate a relativism about facts or values.

Scholars from different fields understand the relationship between facts and values somewhat differently. In disciplines like physics and mathematics, which enjoy a broad consensus on terminology and procedure, the distinction between facts and values is generally taken to be unproblematic. In the social sciences, however, controversy rages over the interdependence of the two. Further study of these basically philosophical issues is strongly recommended here.

CHAPTER HIGHLIGHTS

Two common misconceptions about value were discussed:

1. The first mistake is the idea that "hard fact" will come to the rescue to settle disputes. Often it won't. That's because what a fact is depends upon what authorities we acknowledge to determine what is a fact.
2. The second mistake is believing that criticism is an expression of dislike. It may not be. A person's use of standards of criticism need not mean that he or she personally cares about these standards. Professional coffee tasters might personally prefer tea.

Related Chapters in This Text   **7** Presuppositions
8 Feelings, Facts, and Logic
9 Authority

T E S T   Y O U R S E L F

One reason that the characterization "hard" seems so appropriate for facts is that the way we conceive of facts is in opposition to such "soft" things as wishes, hopes, feelings, and beliefs.

Let's consider what is recognized by people in most, if not all, cultures of this globe to be a fact: beheading is fatal to humans. Suppose examples 1 through 7 below to be true. Now check any of them that you think disprove the statement that beheading is fatal to humans.

_____ 1. John feels that beheading is not fatal to humans.
_____ 2. Sam hopes that beheading is not fatal to humans.
_____ 3. Mary wishes that beheading were not fatal to humans.
_____ 4. Harry believes that beheading is not fatal to humans.
_____ 5. Jack is firmly convinced that beheading is not fatal to humans.
_____ 6. Sue suspects that beheading is not fatal to humans.
_____ 7. As far as Howard is concerned, beheading is not fatal to humans; although he is willing to let us believe what we will.

We hope that you agree that none of them bear on the issue of whether beheading is fatal. What does this then say about the relationship between what we agree are facts and our feeling, hoping, wishing, believing, intuiting, suspecting, or otherwise having an opinion?

CHAPTER 13

BENEFITS AND COSTS

Advocates commonly assure us that what they
propose is the most beneficial choice. Their rivals
make counterproposals that they claim will pay off
better. Such claims and counterclaims are common
in controversies and having a way to evaluate
them is a practical necessity. This chapter contains
such a procedure.

*Nobody buys pebbles which can be picked up
on the beach, but diamonds sell high.*

— A. Philip Randolph

Disagreements normally involve benefit/cost issues. Do it my way, people assure us, and it will pay off. The analytic technique described in this chapter will enable you to dissect such claims.

THREE DIMENSIONS

For purposes of analysis, you can sort **benefits** or **costs** into the following types:

1. divisible/indivisible,
2. absolute/positional, and
3. substantial/symbolic.

Sometimes all three distinctions are useful in analyzing a controversy. In other cases, only one or two of the distinctions are helpful. Let's see how to put them to work.

STEP 1

List benefit claims and counterclaims.

Select a controversy that you want to analyze. Then begin your bene-fit/cost analysis by simply listing the benefits that disputants promise if we follow their advice. (You may not think these promises are all that bene-ficial but list them anyway.)

Here is an example extracted from *Taking Sides: Clashing Views on Con-troversial Moral Issues,* Fifth edition (Dushkin, Guilford, CT, 1996), pp. 112–123. It concerns whether commerce in body parts should be permitted. One disputant, Merrill Matthews Jr., argues that we should permit a market in body parts. His opponent, Stephen G. Post, flatly rejects such commerce.

What are the chief benefits Matthews claims will result if we follow his counsel? How about Post? Here is what they tell us.

Chief Claimed Benefits

Matthews's Proposal: Permit commerce in body parts.	Post's Proposal: Reject such commerce.
Claimed benefit: Permits those providing organs for transplant to receive financial compensation.	**Claimed benefit:** Helps prevent proliferation of poorer-quality organs.
Claimed benefit: Minimizes medical paternalism and puts choices in the hands of people.	**Claimed benefit:** Will prevent a decline in moral idealism.
Claimed benefit: Increases organ availability.	**Claimed benefit:** Will prevent the poor from being exploited for the benefit of the wealthy.

Having constructed the list, we can use our distinctions to appraise it. What follows defines our types, then puts them to work.

Divisible and Indivisible Benefits

Those that can be had by some and not by others are called **divisible benefits.** Consumer goods like cars, clothing, and housing are divisible benefits. Some own a new Dodge Viper, others make do with a battered Hyundai. Nonmaterial benefits can also be divisible. Some people enjoy love and support from their parents while others have to do without.

Indivisible benefits are those that, because it is impractical to restrict access, must benefit all if they benefit any. The ozone layer that protects the planet from ultraviolet radiation provides such a benefit. It prevents worldwide catastrophe, and that ultimately benefits everyone.

Costs work the same way as benefits. Divisible costs are those that can be paid by some while others pay nothing. In the United States, federal income tax works like that. Some millionaires, for instance, pay no income tax whatsoever. Indivisible costs, on the other hand, must be paid by all if they are paid by any. If the ozone layer is damaged and ultraviolet radiation wreaks havoc on agriculture, for example, everyone ultimately pays. In the long run, there is no practical way of avoiding this cost.

 WATCH OUT FOR THIS!

It might be tempting to conclude that there are very few indivisible costs and benefits. Throughout the centuries, however, prophets and sages have insisted that our lives and our fortunes are more interconnected with others than we realize. As the poet John Donne (1573–1631) observed in one of his *Devotions*, "No man is an Iland intire of it selfe."

The divisible/indivisible classification should not be thought of as black or white. Think of it as a continuum such as the one illustrated.

It is unsurprising if you disagree with the placement of some of the items above. How divisible specific benefits (or costs) are is, itself, a matter

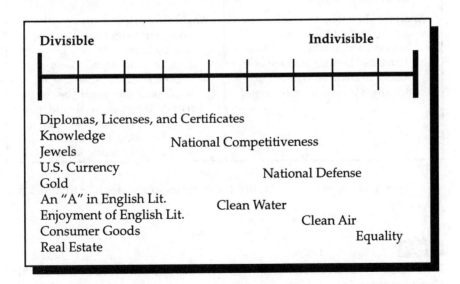

of controversy. Environmentalists, for example, might want to move "clean water" and "clean air" more toward the indivisible side of the continuum. Those contemptuous of "tree hugging" might want to move these same benefits to the left. Differences in perspective and values are what is behind such disagreements. Keep such differences in mind.

For practice, let's try classifying two of the three benefits claimed by the antagonists in the body parts commerce controversy.

Divisible/Indivisible Analysis

Matthews's Proposal: Permit commerce in body parts.	Post's Proposal: Reject such commerce.
Benefit Claimed: Permits those providing organs for transplant to receive financial compensation. **Analysis:** Such compensation is a divisible benefit. Only those parting with a kidney, or their surviving relatives, will be paid. At present, only the medical professionals dealing with the organ transplant receive monetary compensation.	**Benefit Claimed:** Will help prevent proliferation of poorer-quality organs. **Analysis:** Preventing the proliferation of poorer-quality organs is a divisible benefit, but it is not clear who, specifically, would gain. It involves the luck of the draw.
Benefit Claimed: Minimizes medical paternalism and puts choices in the hands of people. **Analysis:** Minimizing medical paternalism and increasing individual choice are presented as indivisible benefits that advantage society as a whole. Whether that is actually the case is controversial.	**Benefit Claimed:** Helps prevent a decline in moral idealism. **Analysis:** Opponents of a market in body parts argue such commerce will undermine human generosity. This, they maintain, would impose the indivisible cost of weakening the moral fiber of the nation. Whether we should agree with that assessment is open to question. Also, how much help would it give moral idealism?

Now you are ready to classify the benefits in the dispute that you are assessing.

STEP 2

Determine if the promised benefits (or costs) are divisible or indivisible. Compare your assessment with what the contending advocates claim.

Remember, disputants often assure us, what they advocate is in everyone's interest. But is it really? Here is an indicator that alerts us that divisible benefits or costs may be misrepresented as indivisible:

   Disputants employ reifications that obscure those who benefit and those who pay. To reify something means to treat abstractions like "America," "the people," or "management" as if they were concrete, even living, things (see chapter 3).

Absolute and Positional Benefits

Now let's turn to the second of our classifications: **absolute and positional benefits**. Characteristics of absolute benefits:

- They retain their value for individuals no matter how many other people enjoy them.
- They need not give advantage over others.
- They don't depend upon someone else's sense of value.
- They are most commonly regarded as ends in themselves rather than as means to other ends.

Absolute benefits often relate to passions, commitments, and habits of the heart. A hug from a loved one, a caring word, delight in the song of a bird, the majestic sight of a roaring sea—these are absolute benefits. Other examples of absolute benefits might be these—a love letter, a high school ring, a fraternity or sorority pin.

Here, in contrast, are the characteristics of positional benefits:

- Their worth depends upon scarcity.
- They give advantage over other people.
- They depend on other people's sense of value.
- They are commonly regarded as means to other ends.

Grades, a diploma, a license to practice medicine, American currency, precious metals, exotic gems—all of these are positional benefits. Each would be worthless if they could be had for the asking. Each gives their possessor advantages over others. Each depends on large numbers of people agreeing that they are worthwhile. Each is commonly regarded as a means to other ends.

Like the divisible/indivisible distinction, this classification is not a black-or-white one. Benefits are more or less absolute or positional, as illustrated in the following chart.

This chart reorganizes the same items found in the divisible/indivisible benefit chart. And just as with that distinction, individuals will vary in their judgments as to whether a benefit is absolute or positional. In fact, that kind of difference of opinion is what some controversies boil down to.

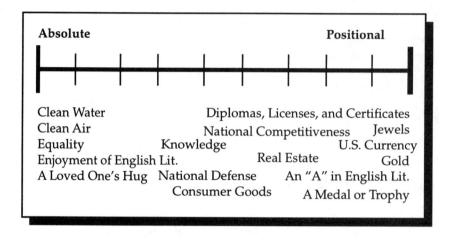

Now let's reexamine the commerce in body parts controversy using this distinction.

Absolute/Positional Analysis

Matthews's Proposal: Permit commerce in body parts.	Post's Proposal: Reject such commerce.
Claimed Benefit: Permits those providing organs for transplant to receive financial compensation.	**Claimed Benefit:** Will help prevent proliferation of poorer-quality organs.
Analysis: Financial compensation is a positional benefit. Scarcity will affect price received. Advantages would go to those with the most money. Organs would go to the highest bidder. Temptation for unloving relatives to look at Uncle Henry as a possible windfall if he would just hurry up and die.	**Analysis:** The fear is that the possibility of substantial benefit will tempt people to sell shoddy "merchandise." This temptation is largely eliminated if the reward for organ donation remains absolute.
Claimed Benefit: Minimizes medical paternalism and puts choices in the hands of people.	**Claimed Benefit:** Helps prevent a decline in moral idealism.
Analysis: Medical paternalism is presented as an absolute cost, or evil, in and of itself. Thus its elimination is presented as an absolute benefit—an end in itself. Do you worry about medical paternalism?	**Analysis:** Preventing such a decline is presented as desirable, or good, in itself. Thus, it is argued to be an absolute benefit.

Using the above as an example, try this distinction on the controversy of your choice by executing Step 3.

Determine if promised benefits are absolute or positional.

Remember, make your own assessment. Then compare your appraisal with the contending advocate's claims.

Substantial and Symbolic Benefits

This is the third and last of our classifications. Benefits (or costs) can also be classified as symbolic or substantial. If something is recognized as valuable across a variety of groups, it is a **substantial benefit**. U.S. currency, for instance, is recognized as valuable around the world. People of nearly every culture want dollars. Even sworn enemies of the United States covet our currency. That is what makes it a substantial benefit. Gold, diamonds, and platinum are, similarly, substantial benefits. Their worth is almost universally recognized.

Here are some additional examples of substantial benefits:

- a twenty-five carat, blue diamond wedding ring
- a new Porsche
- a family portrait by Rembrandt

In contrast, **symbolic benefits** are seen as valuable only by members of a restricted group. Consider the rank of Grand Knight of the Knights of Columbus. It has little significance for anyone who is not a member of the Knights of Columbus, where it is highly admired. Such restricted recognition makes the rank a symbolic benefit. A pack of old love letters might be another example of a symbolic benefit. They may have value for only two people in the world—the ones who exchanged them.

There is a tendency to take symbolic benefits too lightly. Don't. They can be enormously important to certain people. It's just that this importance is recognized only within a restricted community.

Here are some other symbolic benefits:

- an inexpensive wedding ring
- a plastic model of a Porsche: the very first model you ever assembled yourself
- a photo of your family

Notice how these are similar yet importantly different from the examples given for substantial benefits.

WATCH OUT FOR THIS!

When disputants stress symbolic benefits, consider that they may be exploiting commitment to a community or a cause. This maneuver is common in business, for example, where a letter of praise, a plaque, or a pat on the back often substitutes for a raise. Employees motivated by these symbolic benefits are "team players." Those that balk "have an attitude." Meanwhile, in the privacy of the executive suite, these same executives often reward themselves with lucrative stock options or cash bonuses.

Symbolic and substantial benefits also are best thought of as on a continuum, such as the one illustrated.

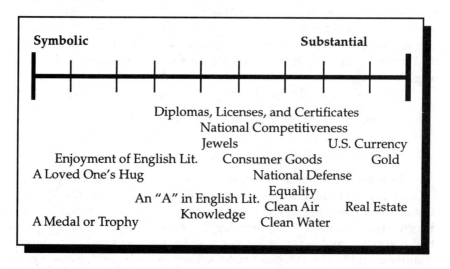

Now we reexamine the commerce in body parts controversy, using this distinction. It can serve as an example for your analysis.

Symbolic/Substantial Analysis

Proposal 1: Permit commerce in body parts.	**Proposal 2: Reject such commerce.**
Claimed Benefit: Permits those providing organs for transplant to receive financial compensation.	**Claimed Benefit:** Will help prevent proliferation of poorer-quality organs.
Analysis: Financial compensation is a substantial benefit. Shifting from a symbolic reward for organ donation to a money reward devalues communal commitments.	**Analysis:** There is not enough experience with commercial organ transplants to establish a widely recognized quality scale. ("Prime," "Choice," "Institutional," that sort of thing) That seems to move this claimed benefit into the symbolic realm.
Claimed Benefit: Minimizes medical paternalism and puts choices in the hands of people.	**Claimed Benefit:** Will help prevent a decline in moral idealism.
Analysis: Only within a limited community is such paternalism a concern. Its minimization is thus a symbolic benefit.	**Analysis:** This is a symbolic benefit that appeals to a limited segment of the population. After all, ideas of moral idealism differ markedly from culture to culture, group to group.

You are now ready to carry out the last step of your benefit/cost analysis.

STEP 4

Determine if promised benefits are substantial or symbolic.

Remember to compare your assessment with what the contending advocates claim. That's when things get interesting.

A LAST WORD ABOUT COSTS

It is important to reemphasize that the typology just given applies to costs as well as benefits. There are:

- Divisible and indivisible costs:
  Destroy the ozone layer and it costs us all. Destroy my car and it costs me.

- Absolute and positional costs:
  Lose a loved one and personal desolation isn't much diminished if many others suffer a similar loss. Lose 10 percent of your income and the impact is much diminished if many others have lost 10 percent of theirs.
- Symbolic and substantial costs:
  Loss of face versus loss of income illustrates this difference.

Cost analysis illuminates controversies in startling ways. Exactly who pays and in what "currency" are often the last things disputants want to talk about. They should be one of the first things you look at.

LIMITATIONS

OF THIS APPROACH   We attempted in this chapter to give an example of analysis that, despite its complexity, is in reality even more complex than could be dealt with in a few charts. But you must begin somewhere. Despite the charts, there is no easy symmetry between costs and benefits.

Also, our approach tends to minimize how much individual perspective influences what is considered a cost or a benefit. Recognizing this element is important.

CHAPTER HIGHLIGHTS

To better understand disputes, ask:

- Does the dispute involve benefits (or costs) and, if so, for whom?
- What type of benefits (or costs) are they: Divisible or indivisible, absolute or positional, symbolic or substantial?
- Is misclassification going on? In other words, is one or another disputant claiming or implying that benefits (or costs) are of one type when they are of another?

If the answer is "yes" for any of these questions, you can be reasonably certain that there is more going on than meets the eye.

Related Chapters   **9** Authority
in This Text   **16** The Nature of Consensus
     17 The Nature of Society

T E S T   Y O U R S E L F

This activity requires classifying benefits or costs. Decide if the listed benefits or costs are more divisible or indivisible, absolute or positional, symbolic or substantial. Circle the area of the continuum you judge appropriate. Item Number 1 provides an example.

TYPE OF BENEFIT OR COST?	Divisible	Indivisible	Absolute	Positional	Symbolic	Substantial
1. A $5,000 salary bonus.	⊖			⊖		⊖
2. Your ten-year-old child plays a piano recital in the school talent show.						
3. Your ten-year-old child plays a piano recital in sold-out Carnegie Hall.						
4. Saving the humpbacked whale from extinction.						
5. Contracting AIDS as a result of illegal drug use.						
6. Contracting AIDS as a result of a transfusion.						
7. Repairing the ozone layer.						
8. Becoming a 32nd degree Mason (the highest rank in the Free and Accepted Masons—a worldwide secret fraternal order).						

CHAPTER **14**

RESPONSIBILITY

Who should be blamed or praised? Who most deserves help? Are we wasting sympathy or public money on people who are just getting what they deserve? To what extent is anyone responsible for who they are or what they do? Are we blaming people for being victims? Despite much scientific research and even more philosophical speculation, these still are open questions. Nevertheless, many arguments hinge on assumptions about personal freedom and responsibility.

Liberty means responsibility. That is why most men dread it.

—George Bernard Shaw

$\mathbf{A}$ssumptions about responsibility are centrally important in analyzing many disputes. Responsibility figures into disputes as issues of guilt, fault, or blame. Consider the present welfare debate. On one side are those who argue that much of the blame for the present situation rests with individuals who prefer indolence to a job, provided that the welfare check arrives regularly. The other side responds that unemployment has more to do with massive changes in the economy that have resulted in not enough jobs to go around and many other considerations. The first argument focuses fault and blame on individuals; the second points to societal issues that individuals cannot control. Both arguments hinge on assumptions about responsibility.

Another example is the controversy about how homosexuality should be regarded. In *Taking Sides: Clashing Views on Controversial Social Issues,* Eighth edition (Guilford, CT: Dushkin, 1994) pp. 76–93, Richard D. Mohr argues that homosexuality should be accepted because gay men and lesbians do not choose to be the way they are; that is, sexual orientation does not seem to be a question of free and deliberate choice. His opponent, Dennis Prager, acknowledges the relevance of the question of choice but procedes to utterly ignore it.

Conditions of Responsibility

Under what conditions is an individual ordinarily thought to be personally responsible? Generally, the answer is only when he or she is believed to have done something or brought it about *freely* and *deliberately.*

But there is extensive disagreement concerning how free and deliberate human behavior really is. Let's briefly review various opinions.

Some maintain that human behavior is so hemmed in by biological and social restrictions that responsibility and blame are severely limited. A few even argue that such restrictions totally eliminate personal freedom and responsibility. In this extreme view, nature and/or nurture rules us, taking us totally beyond responsibility. (Ask yourself, "Why do these people bother to argue?" Since, if they are correct, there's no point in trying to do anything.)

A more moderate view asserts that people can, in fact, freely choose the course of their lives, but only if their basic needs for things like love, acceptance, security, and nourishment have been at least minimally met. In this perspective, the only people who can truly be responsible are those who have fully satisfied these deficiency needs.

Finally, there are those who argue that, barring abnormalities, human behavior is entirely the consequence of individual choices. From this point of view, all normal human beings are fully and personally responsible for who they are and how they behave.

These differing opinions are graphically represented on a continuum:

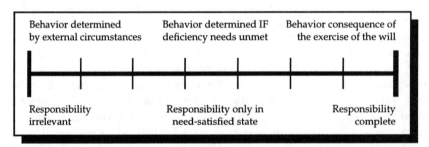

Once again, why is any of this relevant to analyzing disputes? Because many disagreements explicitly, or by inference, involve laying blame, assigning rewards, deciding who deserves help or who deserves praise, and so forth. These matters, in turn, hinge on **explicit** or **implied assumptions** about freedom and responsibility.

Now let's move on to applying these thoughts to dispute analysis. The first thing to remember is that disputants seldom announce their assumptions about responsibility. (Indeed, they may be unaware of making any!) Their suppositions, although commonly buried in other rhetoric, are indicators of whether the dispute is concerned with

☑ who, or what, deserves blame

☑ who merits praise or reward

☑ who deserves help or assistance

So, in analyzing any dispute ask, "Are such issues involved?" For additional clues, look for judgmental terms such as "should" or "ought." They generally indicate that a dispute involves assumptions about freedom and responsibility.

Consider the present heated debate about whether or not to eliminate government aid to unwed mothers and their babies. One side argues that such aid encourages irresponsibility and welfare dependency. Their adversaries claim that eliminating this aid is heartless and stupid. Both are making assumptions about freedom and responsibility. How can we know that? Because the conflict is about who, or what, is to blame when children have children. It is also about who, in turn, deserves help or assistance. And both sides argue in terms of "oughts" and "shoulds." All of this alerts us to the fact that the dispute involves assumptions about freedom and responsibility.

Now you are ready to carry out the first step of your own analysis.

STEP 1

Determine if the dispute involves assumptions about responsibility.

Remember that disputants seldom tell us openly what they are assuming about responsibility. Look for evidence of their conviction.

Freely and Deliberately Choosing?

Consider, once again, the heated national debate about curtailing or eliminating government aid to unwed mothers and their babies. Hard-line opponents argue for eliminating such assistance because it unintentionally rewards teenage girls for having babies out of wedlock. The only way to stop such undesirable behavior, say these critics, is to allow those who choose pregnancy to "enjoy" the *full* consequences of that choice. They concede that, like innocent civilians killed in vitally necessary bombing raids, babies will receive "collateral damage." But they argue that there simply is no other practical way to discourage the birth of ever more such babies in the future.

What is being assumed about teenage girls' understanding of freedom and responsibility issues here? The assumptions are that these young women who have become pregnant know how to avoid pregnancy, how hard it is to get a decent job, how scarce inexpensive day care is, how unlikely it is that the father will assume his responsibilities, and so forth. Plus, and this is crucial, that in spite of knowing all of these things, such young people *freely* and *deliberately* choose either to risk pregnancy or to deliberately conceive.

What follows logically from these assumptions? That when a child is born who cannot be nurtured as it should be, the mother and the father are personally to blame because they freely chose to risk parenthood. Thus, unlike persons who have been victimized through no fault of their own, these parents have no legitimate claim on public assistance. The blameless baby does have a claim, but, these critics argue, there is no practical way to help the baby without also aiding at least the mother, thus encouraging further irresponsibility.

Those in favor of continuing the Aid to Dependent Children program respond that if we knew enough about these girls' home lives, the mean streets they walk, their desperate need to love and be loved, their naive view of what it takes to raise a baby, their lack of real opportunity for a better life, and their immaturity, we would understand why they stumble into pregnancy. At the very least, there is a question of priorities. Is the life of an innocent child worth less than the "lesson" taught to its mother by withholding welfare?

Who, or what, is assumed responsible in this interpretation? Fault, it is claimed, lies in a socioeconomic system that, because of a maldistribution of wealth, forces people into a desperate culture of poverty. Ensnared in this web of misery, which they do not understand, much less control, children *do* have children, these advocates say, but they can hardly be said to have really *freely* and *deliberately* made a choice. They are, it is argued, actually victims of their circumstances. And their babies are also victims. So both parent and child have legitimate claims on public assistance.

It is unimportant whether you agree or disagree with either of these positions. It is just an example. What *is* important is that you be able to tell when disputes involve assumptions about:

• Who has what options?
• Who is aware of their options?
• Who is in control?
• Who is not?

Now you are ready for Step 2.

STEP 2

Identify who, or what, the disputants think is responsible.

Remember, in making this identification, to ask:

• Who is portrayed as having no choice?
• What is assumed about range of, and knowledge of, choices?
• What assumptions are being made about control?

These questions are crucial.

Are Assumptions about Responsibility Supported by Evidence?

Many arguments hinge on false, or at least dubious, assertions regarding responsibility. Here is a real-life example. To adjudicate a highly controversial school desegregation case, Pennsylvania Commonwealth judge Doris Smith established a blue-ribbon panel to plan a remedy for disparities in achievement and opportunity found in the Philadelphia public schools. The team consulted with thousands of people before issuing its findings. Then they reported to Judge Smith,

> The School District of Philadelphia has been confronted with obstacles plaguing most urban school districts in the United States: declining budgets, deteriorating buildings, increasing numbers of students with special needs, an exodus of middle-class families, divisive local and state politics, declining levels of student achievement, top-heavy bureaucracies and union conflicts, as well as violence, vandalism, health care needs, absenteeism, teenage pregnancy and dropout levels that make teaching and learning a secondary focus in the City's schools.

Significantly, the team then added,

> Student achievement in the School District of Philadelphia has also been limited by low expectations spawned by the myth that poverty limits what students can learn. Again and again, in public meetings and in focus groups with teachers, administrators and public officials, the Team members hear that children are "broken," not by poor schools, but by life circumstances including poverty, health problems, emotional and substance abuse, and the existence of teenage, single-parent families. Blaming low achievement on these "powerless to control" forces is dangerous because it fosters a lack of accountability . . . the responsibility of the School District is to ensure that high-quality teaching and learning occurs in every school.

Note that the team claims it is a "myth" that poverty limits what students can learn. Thus the "School District" is accountable when high-quality learning does not take place in every school. But is the panel right in assuming that School District educators have enough control over critical factors to "ensure high-quality learning"?

Here is where you have to do some library research. (See the Appendix for a guide.) When we review research on the subject of school achievement, two studies stand out. The most extensive study came out of the Civil Rights Act of 1964, when Congress ordered the Commissioner of Education to study this very issue. Harvard professor of education James Coleman was selected to head the study team. Coleman's massive survey of 600,000 children in all 50 states pointed to the critical importance of *nonschool* factors, particularly, family background, in variations in school achievement. The study summarized this finding this way:

> One implication stands out above all: That schools bring little influence to bear on a child's achievement that is independent of his background and

general social context; and that this very lack of an independent effect means that the inequalities imposed on children by their home, neighborhood, and peer environment are carried along to become the inequalities with which they confront adult life at the end of school.

Another massive research project conducted eight years later confirmed Coleman's findings. Christopher Jencks's extensive study of American social differences as they relate to schooling took three years to complete. Like Coleman's study, it revealed that school results are influenced almost solely by the characteristics of the entering children. Jencks's study concluded:

> [C]hildren seem to be far more influenced by what happens at home than what happens in school. They may also be more influenced by what happens on the streets and by what they see on television. Everything else—the school budget, its policies, the characteristics of the teachers—is either secondary or completely irrelevant.

So the two most extensive research studies available directly contradict the assertion that officials of the School District of Philadelphia can fairly be held responsible for schooling failures. Of course, these two studies are not the last word; and new things have been learned about improving teaching and learning since they were completed. Still, it won't do to simply dismiss the importance of nonschool factors as a "myth." School District officials are certainly responsible for ensuring high-quality teaching. But, given what Coleman's and Jencks's research reveals, perhaps they should not also be held responsible for ensuring "high-quality learning."

That brings us to our third and last step.

STEP 3

Consider that disputants' assumptions about responsibility might be wrong.

In analyzing any dispute ask:

- Do the antagonists present evidence to support their assumptions?
- Does research offer contrary evidence regarding who, or what, is responsible?

WATCH OUT FOR THIS!

Disputants often offer no evidence supporting their assumptions about responsibility. Nevertheless, these assumptions are often the very foundation of their argument. If *you* share their opinion, you might be tempted to allow questionable assumptions to pass unexamined, because you don't want to look carefully at your own. Get tough and face that possible threat. Relentlessly ask who is assuming what about responsibility. Then question the basis for those assumptions. Are they supported by evidence?

CHAPTER HIGHLIGHTS

Controversies often rest on different conceptions of responsibility. These, in turn, hinge on assumptions about personal freedom and accountability. These assumptions are important even if many of them are only implied. Some assumptions about freedom and responsibility might be unsupported by evidence. So to better understand any dispute ask:

- Does the dispute involve assumptions about freedom and responsibility?
- If so, who, or what, do the disputants assume to be responsible?
- Is there evidence to support either side's assumptions?

LIMITATIONS
OF THIS APPROACH

We have focused almost exclusively on concepts of personal responsibility. We have taken the position that notions of group responsibility or "inherited" guilt ultimately come down to the actions and choices of individuals. Some argue that class membership alone is sufficient for individual guilt. We are not convinced.

Related Chapters in This Text

- **3** Reifications
- **6** Name-Calling
- **7** Presuppositions
- **12** Fact and Value
- **17** The Nature of Society

T E S T   Y O U R S E L F

Evaluate the following statements by estimating how much individual responsibility is implied. Circle the appropriate area of the continuum. Remember, people are ordinarily thought to be personally responsible only when they are believed to have done it or brought something about *freely* and *deliberately*.

Statement	Degree of Responsibility on the Part of the Poor
People who are much too sensitive to demand of cripples that they run races, ask of the poor that they get up and act just like everyone else in society. —Michael Harrington	Responsible ⊢—┼—┼—┼—┼—┼—┤ Not Responsible
Poverty has many roots, but the tap root is ignorance. —Lyndon B. Johnson	Responsible ⊢—┼—┼—┼—┼—┼—┤ Not Responsible
In a change of government, the poor change nothing beyond the change of their masters. —Phaedrus	Responsible ⊢—┼—┼—┼—┼—┼—┤ Not Responsible
It is easy to say that poverty is no crime. No, if it were men wouldn't be ashamed of it. It's a blunder, though, and punished as such. —Jerome K. Jerome	Responsible ⊢—┼—┼—┼—┼—┼—┤ Not Responsible
Poverty is no disgrace, but no honor either. —Yiddish Proverb	Responsible ⊢—┼—┼—┼—┼—┼—┤ Not Responsible

PART 4 METAPROBLEMS

Some critical issues prowl in the background of controversy, often going unrecognized. This section brings to the foreground for examination a sample of the more important of these metaproblems.

This section examines

- how logical errors influence disputes,
- the nature and importance of consensus,
- common assumptions about the nature of society, and
- hidden agendas that perpetuate controversies.

CHAPTER 15

WHAT'S ILLOGICAL?

Have you ever been criticized as "illogical"? Many people accuse those who disagree with them of being so. Sometimes people *do* make errors in **logic**. More often, however, a controversy arises because the disputants' reasoning is based on different assumptions. In this chapter we learn to distinguish what is illogical from what is merely misinformed.

> *Logic commands us far more tyrannically than any master; in disobeying the latter we are made unhappy, in disobeying the former, fools.*
>
> —Blaise Pascal

The most common experience people have with any formalized reasoning process is when they study high school geometry. There they learn to begin with definitions, prove intermediate conclusions, called **lemmas**, and reach final conclusions, called **theorems**. The general pattern is a sequence of statements in which all but the last one are called **premises**, and the last statement is called a **conclusion**. We do not have the space to investigate all of the possible kinds of arguments that can be constructed, so we will focus on the simplest.

THE SYLLOGISM

The **syllogism** has only two premises and one conclusion. Despite its brevity, however, it is useful because longer arguments are built up from syllogisms. And any longer argument that contains an ill-formed syllogism is illogical.

The Structure of a Syllogism

Premise: All men are mortal.
Premise: Sam is a man.
Conclusion: Therefore, Sam is mortal.

Validity and Soundness

An **argument** may be a bad one for two reasons:
1. It is invalid.
2. It is unsound.

An **invalid argument** has a structure that permits false conclusions to be drawn from true premises. An **unsound argument** may be valid but has false premises. Consider the following examples.

Examples	Comments
1. An invalid argument form: Logicians call this invalidity **undistributed middle** with true premises: a. All dogs are mammals. b. All canines are mammals. c. Therefore, all dogs are canines.	1. Note that the premises and conclusion are true. This *form* is invalid, however, because we can substitute other terms in parallel fashion and get clearly false conclusions: a. All oranges are fruit. b. All apples are fruit. c. Therefore, all oranges are apples.
2. A valid argument form with true premises. a. All dogs are canines. b. All canines are mammals. c. Therefore, all dogs are mammals.	2. A valid argument form guarantees us the truth of the conclusion if the premises are true. Since the premises are *true* and the argument form a *valid* one, this argument is also *sound*.
3. The form of a valid argument is independent of the truth of the premises. Consider this unsound argument: a. Guernseys are snakes. b. Snakes give milk. c. Therefore, guernseys give milk.	3. False premises make the argument unsound. They do not guarantee the truth of the conclusion. Using false premises, it is possible to construct all sorts of logical nonsense, e.g.: a. All flood waters play the guitar. b. All guitar players eat hubcaps. c. Therefore, all flood waters eat hubcaps.

The practical upshot is this. You may object to an argument on the grounds that it is invalid. This means it doesn't really connect its premises to its conclusion, no matter whether or not the premises or the conclusion are individually recognized to be true. Or you may object to an argument on the grounds that it is unsound. That is, despite its being in good form—connecting its premises to its conclusion—one or more of its premises are false.

The truth of the premises of an argument—unlike its form—is not apparent from the argument itself. It may be a matter of dispute whether the premises of an argument are true. The truth of premises must be ascertained by methods external to the argument in question, that is, further argument, research, recourse to authority, and so forth. A controversy, then, may result either from invalid argument or from unsound argument.

COMMON LOGICAL ERRORS

It is useful to be able to recognize several kinds of logical errors. These are traditionally described in a technical language that can be somewhat complex. Here, instead, are examples of the most common errors. For each type, there is a simple example that easily reveals the error, then a more realistic example.

1. Undistributed Middle

    a. Apples are fruits. Oranges are fruits. So apples are oranges.
    b. Sam reads Karl Marx, so he must be a communist because communists read Marx.

2. Unwarranted Converse

    a. All dogs are warm-blooded. Your pet is warm-blooded. So it must be a dog.
    b. John must be a businessman, since businessmen support immigration and so does John.

3. Some to All

    a. Some animals are meat eaters. Your pet is an animal. So it must be a meat eater.
    b. Some businessmen support unrestricted immigration. John is a businessman, so he must support unrestricted immigration.

4. Negating the Antecedent

    a. All oranges are fruit. Since this is not an orange, it is not a fruit.
    b. Since union members oppose unrestricted immigration and John is not a union member, he does not oppose unrestricted immigration.

LIMITATIONS

OF THIS APPROACH   This chapter restricts itself to syllogisms and leaves un-
mentioned the many other more sophisticated approaches
to logic. One must start somewhere. Understanding these
basics is only a first step.

CHAPTER HIGHLIGHTS

It is important not to confuse whether an argument is illogical or merely
misinformed. A valid argument form assures us that if our premises are
true, our conclusion is true. However, a valid argument may have false
premises. Whether the premises are true has to be determined from external
evidence. Misinformation makes the conclusion questionable as fact but
does not make it illogical. Even logical people can make factual mistakes.

Related Chapters   **8** Feelings, Facts, and Logic
in This Text   **10** Operationalizing

T E S T   Y O U R S E L F

Evaluate the arguments below. Rewrite them as syllogisms. Determine whether they are valid and/or sound. There may be an unstated premise. Finally, identify any fallacies.

1. Sally is studying calculus. She must want to be an engineer. Engineers use calculus all the time.
2. Jack must be a conservative, since he reads the very conservative *National Review* regularly.
3. My brother's goat gives milk. Your goat must give milk, too.
4. All Chinese are communists. Fred is a communist, so he must be Chinese.
5. Real men don't eat quiche. Sally is not a real man. So Sally eats quiche.

CHAPTER 16

THE NATURE OF CONSENSUS

If you need the help of other people to get things done, you had better worry about consensus. **Consensus** is group agreement in judgment, belief, or opinion. In a controversy, disputants try to build consensus for their particular position among the uncommitted. Triviality, evasiveness, and sloganizing are a frequent consequence. This chapter explains the dynamics of consensus building and how it both reshapes and distorts public controversies. The chapter also provides specifics on how to evaluate consensus in its three dimensions.

It is by universal misunderstanding that all agree.

—Charles Baudelaire

Democracy assigns critical importance to agreement. After all, the voters ultimately must support action on controversial issues. In a pluralistic democracy, however, consensus tends to be both short-lived and shallow. Moreover, disputes are often deformed and trivialized by the necessity of obtaining or maintaining this broad, but shallow, agreement. Election rhetoric abundantly demonstrates this.

THREE DIMENSIONS OF CONSENSUS

Consensus among a group of people can be evaluated in three dimensions: breadth, depth, and span.

Breadth of Consensus: On a Specific Issue, How Many Members of the Group Agree?

Lets take, for example, group opinion on traffic laws. A great majority of people agree that, in general, traffic laws should be followed. The breadth here is substantial but superficial. Some, however, exempt themselves from obeying stop signs on lightly traveled roads while others do not. Many go far faster than the speed limit when it seems safe while others will obey the law even on a deserted four-lane highway. So, even in issues where principle is generally honored, specific practice is open for personal decision. Thus, not only the breadth but the depth of consensus is an important consideration. What is that?

131

Depth of Consensus: Given Consensus on a Specific Issue, How Many Details Are Agreed To?

People may share consensus on a specific issue, for example, that teenage pregnancies should be reduced, but disagree when it comes to how that should come about. Some may advocate more sex education; others the distribution of birth control devices; others still, abstinence. Thus the initial consensus dissolves into competing proposals for action.

Depth of consensus explains much about disputes. Consider the political argumentation during elections. Citizens often complain that political candidates avoid discussing issues and overindulge in sloganizing. But savvy candidates know that slogans are a mechanism for creating consensus (even if temporary) and that getting more specific will risk destroying it (temporary, seemingly deep, consensus means votes). Voters may agree with slogans but usually have differing ideas on the details (see chapter 2).

Span of Consensus

The third essential dimension of consensus, as we have said, is called the span. Span is a measure of *how many different issues* a group agrees upon. Recognizing that the United States is a pluralistic society, most Americans do not find it unusual—as many foreign visitors to the United States do—that people will often live in the same neighborhood, go to school, and work with others of different religions, occupations, educational backgrounds, and family histories; even with people of different ethnic and racial memberships. It is this span of consensus that defines American pluralism. Perhaps a pluralistic society is possible only because people have learned to accommodate to the fact that on any given issue broad consensus can be expected to be shallow.

Remember, span of consensus is different from breadth of consensus. Span looks at *numbers* of *different* issues agreed upon (however superficially); breadth of consensus looks at how many people line up on a specific issue.

Spans of consensus define various coalitions in American pluralism. Knowing something about these coalitions is essential for analyzing public affairs. For instance, the Gallup organization uses the extent to which people agree on a range of values (things like belief in God or that America works for them) to divide Americans into 11 distinct voter groups. Polling of these groups then allows the Gallup organization reliably to predict national election results when only a small percentage of the vote has been tallied.

Here is a snapshot of Gallup's American pluralism. You can use this table to make rough predictions of how the listed value-coalitions might line up on controversial issues. Remember, each of these groups represents a *span of consensus*.

Republican-Oriented Groups

Name	Percent of Likely Electorate	Characteristics and Typical Values
Enterprisers	16 percent	Affluent, well-educated, pro-business, antigovernment, worry about deficit
Moralists	14 percent	Middle income, antiabortion, pro-school prayer, pro-military
Upbeats	9 percent	Young, optimistic, strongly patriotic, pro-government, worry about deficit
Disaffecteds	7 percent	Middle-aged, alienated, pessimistic, antigovernment and antibusiness, pro-military

Democrat-Oriented Groups

Name	Percent of Likely Electorate	Characteristics and Typical Values
60s Democrats	11 percent	Well-educated, identify with 1960s peace, environmental, and civil rights movements
New Dealers	15 percent	Older, middle-income, pro-union, protectionist, pro-government
Passive Poor	6 percent	Older, religious, patriotic, pro-social spending, anticommunist
Partisan Poor	9 percent	Young, little faith in America or politics, worry about unemployment
Followers	4 percent	Middle-aged, well-educated, nonreligious, nonmilitant, pro-personal freedoms
Seculars	9 percent	Middle-aged, alienated, pessimistic, antigovernment and antibusiness, pro-military

Nonvoting Group

Name	Percent of Likely Electorate	Characteristics and Typical Values
Bystanders	0 percent	Young, poorly educated, 82 percent white, many unmarried, worried about unemployment and threat of war

Gallup's data suggests that the terms "liberal" and "conservative" are of little help in understanding the complexities of public controversies. In fact, these terms are slogans that often obscure important differences among people.

 # WATCH OUT FOR THIS!

We sometimes naively expect that by "getting clearer" we can re-solve conflicts. But pushing for greater clarity and specificity and probing for hidden disagreements could easily undermine consen-sus. If we all really understood one another, we might disagree even more. For this reason, skilled disputants spend a lot of time making issues appear simpler than they really are. Where commit-ment is unclear, obscurity is functional. Superficiality, vagueness, and sloganizing in a dispute can be the means for establishing and maintaining a broad, if shallow, consensus.

TOOLS FOR EVALUATING CONSENSUS ISSUES

Among the tools for evaluating issues of consensus are the consensus curve and analytic procedure.

The Consensus Curve

The consensus curve (below) examines the slogan "love and honor" found in many traditional marriage ceremonies. It shows how that slogan initially enjoys broad but shallow consensus; but fewer and fewer agree on how it should translate into action in specific instances. As we add "by" statements (by compromising on money matters, by tolerating obnoxious in-laws, etcetera), more and more people in the family circle say, "Count me out." In the end, only a relatively narrow group of people share deep (detailed) consensus on what "love and honor" mean in specific instances. This group, it is to be hoped, still includes the bride and groom!

We can see why marital and family squabbles break out as couples try to reach agreement on the details of their initial commitment to "love and honor" each other.

Consensus Curve

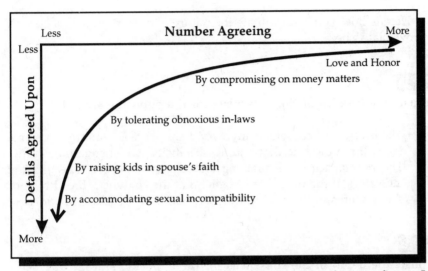

Public disputes work in the same way. Consider the next figure. It illustrates consensus on the value of promoting national literacy. Notice how each specific regarding how to accomplish this goal reduces the breadth of consensus. Each new specific sparks a new dispute. In pluralistic societies, in particular, breadth of consensus shrinks as we add details of implementation.

Consensus on Promoting National Literacy

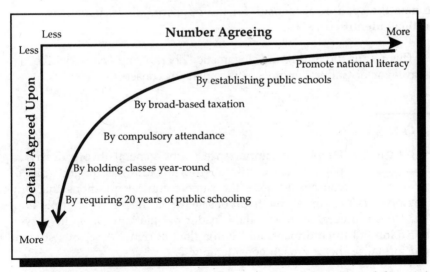

This is the critical point to understand: *Any* elaboration of the original slogan risks creating a controversy.

The Analytic Procedure

Here is how you can evaluate the nature of a consensus on a specific controversial issue:

STEP 1

Estimate the breadth of the consensus for the opposing sides.

- The breadth of consensus involves a simple head count on a single issue. But anticipate that adding specificity will change the count.
- The persistence of sloganizing and the avoidance of specifics are indicators of the proponent's belief that the consensus breadth he or she is searching for will quickly evaporate if specifics are added.

STEP 2

Estimate the depth of the consensus for the opposing sides.

Remember, consensus has depth when people agree on something in *detail*. Thus, the depth of consensus is probed by examining how many details have been agreed to regarding either means or ends or both.

STEP 3

Estimate the span of consensus for the opposing sides, using the value coalitions identified by Gallup.

This means discarding the sloganistic "liberal" and "conservative" labels in favor of Gallup's more specific spans of consensus.

LIMITATIONS

OF THIS APPROACH   Despite the importance of the general theory described here, practical estimation of breadth, depth, and span of consensus raises the same technical questions that any survey does. Is the survey method consistent? Is the survey sample adequate? Does it accurately reflect the broader population? Does the survey truly explore all three dimensions? Is the data current? A serious student would formalize the approach considerably.

CHAPTER HIGHLIGHTS

Consensus among a group of people can be evaluated in three dimensions:

- Breadth of consensus; the number of people who agree on an issue.
- Depth of consensus; the number of details that are agreed to.
- Span of consensus; the number of issues that are agreed upon.

Normally, as breadth of consensus increases, depth decreases and vice versa. Span of consensus also decreases as details are added. This dynamic encourages superficiality and sloganizing in disputes and often gives the appearance of agreement.

Related Chapters in This Text

- **2** Slogans
- **3** Reification
- **7** Presuppositions
- **13** Benefits and Costs
- **14** Responsibility
- **17** The Nature of Society
- **18** Why Controversies Persist

TEST YOURSELF

Here are some controversial proposals. Refer back to the charts identifying the Gallup coalitions of interest and guestimate how different groups would line up on each of these proposals. List them in the spaces labeled pro and con. What alliances form? (Note: all groups need not be listed. List only those that you think would clearly be pro or con.)

Also consider what would be the breadth and depth of consensus that they might share. Would it matter if more details were provided? (You might try providing some details yourself and see how that might affect consensus.)

a. State vouchers should be issued to help parents who want to opt for private schooling.

    Pro:

    Con:

b. Drug usage should be decriminalized.

    Pro:

    Con:

CHAPTER 17

THE NATURE OF SOCIETY

We're often told that we must obey the rules of society. Whose rules are these? What, exactly, is society anyway and who belongs to it? Most people imagine they have answers to these questions. But even if they do, these answers are often unexamined. Nevertheless, such unconsidered opinions creep into and influence many debates. That is why spotting and understanding them is essential in analyzing disputes.

> *If I go to a restaurant, I am very likely to get*
> *that meal free. But poor people who go to the*
> *same restaurant got to wash dishes to eat. And*
> *I'm the one who can afford it. Explain that,*
> *and then you can explain society.*
>
> —Michael Jordan

Assumptions about "society" greatly influence many controversies. Even when such assumptions are centrally influential, however, they are seldom obvious. This chapter describes how to spot their hidden presence and explains their practical impact on disputes.

MODELS OF SOCIETY

There are three conflicting models of society that most commonly generate controversy. They are

- the consensus model,
- the conflict model, and
- the individualistic model.

The Consensus Model

Most people unthinkingly embrace the **consensus model** of society. In this model, society is assumed to be a harmonious, stable, well-integrated system resembling a living organism. Individuals are presumed to play the same sort of complementary and interdependent roles that nerve, bone, or blood cells play in the body's functioning. Supported by "society," individuals obtain their meaning and importance from it.

The consensus model emphasizes the importance of stability and the desirability of common perceptions, values, and morals. Maintaining the existing social order and integrating individuals into the social structure are centrally important. Social stability is essential. People or activities that do not fit in are regarded as deviant, perhaps even pathological. As the Japanese proverb says, "The nail that sticks up, gets hammered down."

The consensus model largely ignores the possibility of exploitation. By emphasizing social harmony, it obscures the likelihood that people might be competing for the same limited resources or that some individuals gain at the expense of others.

Here is a quotation from the highly influential *A Nation at Risk: The Imperative for Educational Reform*, a report by the National Commission on Excellence in Education (Washington, DC: Superintendent of Documents, U.S. Government Printing Office, 1985, pages 5–6). See if you can spot consensus-model assumptions about the nature of society. Remember, in most controversies, they are implied rather than stated.

> Our Nation is at risk. Our once unchallenged preeminence in commerce, industry, science, and technological innovation is being overtaken by competitors throughout the world. This report is concerned with only one of the many causes and dimensions of the problem, but it is one that undergirds American prosperity, security and civility. We report to the American people that while we can take justifiable pride in what our schools and colleges have historically accomplished and contributed to the United States and the well-being of its people, the educational foundations of our society are presently being eroded by a rising tide of mediocrity that threatens our very future as a Nation and a people....
>
> Our society and its educational institutions seem to have lost sight of the basic purposes of schooling, and of the high expectations and disciplined efforts needed to attain them. This report ... seeks to generate reform of our educational system in fundamental ways and to renew the Nation's commitment to schools and colleges of high quality throughout the length and breadth of our land.

Notice that the authors reify American society. They refer to it as if it were of one mind and one purpose (see chapter 3). For example, the commissioners maintain that "Our society and its educational institutions seem to have lost sight of the basic purposes of schooling." Only in the consensus model does a society have "sight." The commissioners speak of renewing "the Nation's commitment to schools and colleges of high quality." Here again, America is a kind of supersized person that makes commitments. The commissioners also refer to "American prosperity, security and civility" as if one American cannot be prosperous and secure without all Americans achieving the same status. The rest of the report is written in the same manner.

Why is any of this important? Because consensus-model assumptions obscure crucial issues. Which individuals have lost sight of these things? Whose basic purposes are we talking about? Is it "the Nation" that is at risk, the vested interests of a wealthy and powerful class of people, or just the well-being of specific individuals? These and similar questions are obscured.

A presidential commission using the consensus model of society is unsurprising. People in leadership positions frequently invoke the consensus model, perhaps because it downplays, even disguises, differences in wealth and privilege, costs and benefits. Also, it promotes consensus and undercuts dissensus by implying that deviance, dissension, or even criticism of the report are inappropriate, perhaps even disloyal.

The following are indicators that the consensus model is operating in an argument:

☑ Diverse groups of people are referred to as if they were of one mind and one need, for example, America.

☑ Individual needs, aspirations, or perceptions are not mentioned. (See reifications elsewhere in the text.)

☑ Conflicts, antagonisms, and the possibility of exploitation are ignored.

The Conflict Model

The assumption of the **conflict model** is that societies are arenas in which various groups struggle for contradictory goals and compete for limited resources. Accordingly, whenever a special interest group gains power, it tries to preserve control by imposing its own values and understandings on those whom it exploits. Those subscribing to the conflict model claim that this is why societies are arranged so unequally and why injustice is so persistent that it often seems that two societies exist: one rich, the other poor. That was what the famed British prime minister Benjamin Disraeli was referring to when he noted, "I was told that the Privileged and the People formed two nations" (Sybil, 1845).

Notice that while the consensus model stresses communal balance and harmony, the conflict model emphasizes imbalances and disharmonies. Conflicts between groups are understood to be unavoidable; inequalities are inevitable, as is the coercion used to maintain dominance. Hostility, change, and instability are presented as the natural order of things.

How different *A Nation at Risk* would be if written from a conflict perspective. The first paragraph would read something like this:

The wealth and privileges of America's power elite are at risk. The once unchallenged preeminence in commerce, industry, science, and technological innovation of the corporations they own is being overtaken by international competitors. This report is concerned with only one of the many causes and dimensions of the problem, but it is one that undergirds the power elite's prosperity and security. We report, too, that while the privileged can take comfort in how our schools and colleges have further reinforced fundamental inequalities of opportunity for personal development and economic reward in the United States, the educational foundations of this system are presently being eroded by a rising tide of resentment, resistance, and alienation that threatens the very repression and domination that foster and perpetuate privilege.

Like the consensus model, the conflict model relies on reifications; but the conflict model reifies oppositional societal classes rather than the whole society. There are the "privileged" and the "underprivileged," the "advantaged" and the "disadvantaged," the "bourgeoisie" and the "proletariat," the "power elite," and "the poor." These classes of people are depicted as of one mind with one set of needs.

Those seeking reform, change, even revolution, usually employ the conflict model. By accentuating differences in wealth and privilege and costs and benefits, it stimulates dissatisfaction and discontent.

Here are some indicators that the conflict model is operative in a dispute:

☑ Individuality is submerged in reified antagonistic classes or groups.

☑ Oppositional terms are applied as labels.

☑ Class conflicts and antagonisms are emphasized.

The Individualistic Model

The importance of individual differences is stressed in the **individualistic model** of society. The group counts for little. You might recall the famous quote of Henry David Thoreau, the philosopher of individualism, "If a man does not keep pace with his companions, perhaps it is because he hears a different drummer. Let him step to the music he hears, however measured or far away" (Walden, 1854).

Rejecting reifications like "America," the "ruling class," or the "working class," proponents of this view argue that individual differences are the prime consideration. Reifications, they say, should be reduced to the relations and actions of distinctly different individuals. References to things like "America's needs," as in the consensus model, or the "power elite," as in the conflict model, obscure the most important issue of all, namely, which particular person's needs or wants are really at issue?

Let's return to *A Nation At Risk* and see how it might read from an individualistic perspective. Notice how different, even awkward, it is compared to the two previous versions. That is because the individualistic model requires the *elimination* of reifications.

> Certain individual interests are at risk. Some U.S. corporations are being overtaken by foreign competitors. This report is concerned with only one of the many causes and dimensions of this situation, but it is one that undergirds the prosperity and security of these particular Americans. We report to those of you who are interested that while some of us take pride in what schools and colleges have historically contributed to the well-being of these U.S. citizens, the educational foundations of that well-being are presently being eroded. That threatens these particular people's comfort and standard of living.

The individualistic model stresses that it is particular persons who benefit or who pay the costs. Individualistic model partisans insist that reifications won't do. No class or category of people are really that much alike. Suspect that the individualistic model is operative in a dispute when:

☑ Reifications are challenged with demands for specifics.

☑ Individual differences are the focus of attention.

THE TWO-STEP PROCEDURE

Having defined three models of society, now let's put them to work. Here is a two-step procedure for analyzing controversies in terms of assumptions about society.

STEP 1

Identify the model(s) of society assumed by disputants.

This requires deducing the usually implicit definition by using the descriptions and indicators previously provided.

STEP 2

Restate key portions of each disputant's argument using language appropriate to the models of society not favored.

This spotlights key issues that are otherwise ignored. This, indeed, is the procedure followed in our analysis of *A Nation at Risk*.

WATCH OUT FOR THIS!

There is no need to decide which competing image or model of society is right. Just be aware of assumptions about society that disputants bring to the table and know that the argument looks entirely different when competing judgments are substituted.

CHAPTER HIGHLIGHTS

Suppositions about society are often important in analyzing controversies. Even when such suppositions are pivotal to the argument, however, they are seldom conspicuous. This chapter explained how to identify these assumptions and spelled out what they conceal.

Remember, to better understand any dispute ask:

• What, if any, assumptions are made about the nature of society?
• How would the argument be altered if competing assumptions were correct?

LIMITATIONS

OF THIS APPROACH   In pursuing simplicity, we have ignored the fact that many scholars see these models as interacting with one another. For instance, individuals are, to some extent, defined by their social context and still struggle against it.

Related Chapters in This Text

3 Reification
6 Name-Calling
7 Presuppositions
9 Authority
13 Benefits and Costs
16 The Nature of Consensus
18 Why Controversies Persist

T E S T   Y O U R S E L F

See if you can identify the model of society implicit in each of the following quotes. In the appropriate boxes briefly note your reasoning. The first case example provides a model.

Case Example	Individualistic	Conflict	Consensus
1. *In a civilized society we all depend upon each other and our happiness is very much owing to the good opinion of mankind.* Samuel Johnson, quoted in James Boswell's *Life of Samuel Johnson*	No, it emphasizes importance of groups.	No, it does not imply conflict between groups.	Yes, emphasis on inter-dependence.
2. *American schools had to maintain the illusion of democracy in a society where the increasing agglomeration of wealth in the hands of the few was rendering negligible the political power of the many.* David Nasaw, *Schooled to Order.* (What model of society is Nasaw taking for granted?)			
3. *Human life in common is only possible when a majority comes together which is stronger than any separate individual, and which remains united against all separate individuals.* Sigmund Freud, *Civilization and Its Discontents*			
4. *Society looks to higher schools for assistance in understanding its own problems and for light upon the principles underlying their solution.* Agatho Zimmer, FSC, "Changing Concepts in Higher Education since 1700"			
5. *Ein Volk; Ein Reich; Ein Fuhrer!* Nazi unity motto meaning, roughly, "One people, one empire, one leader."			

CHAPTER 18

WHY CONTROVERSIES

PERSIST

Have you ever been pushed into an argument that
you couldn't seem to avoid? You should know that
there are numerous hidden payoffs in starting or
prolonging disputes. In fact, provoking or
maintaining controversies pays off so well that
some people start fights just to reap these benefits.
This chapter explains how that works. It also lays
out steps for clarifying these covert agendas.

A disputant no more cares for the truth than the sportsman for the hare.

—Alexander Pope

People are often dismayed when the leaders of opposing factions profess the desire for peace even as they provoke war. Diplomats may make public declarations of their commitment to peace while armies mobilize. Political leaders in Washington speak of reconciliation while closing down the government. Teachers' unions and school board leaders may express severe misgivings about closing down the schools as they wrangle themselves, inevitably it seems, into a strike. This may look like blatant hypocrisy or sheer stupidity; but, actually, something else is going on.

Wars, and other sorts of conflicts, could be avoided if one side agreed to cave in to the other. "I sincerely wish to put an end to this conflict" has to be understood to mean the following: "I sincerely wish to put an end to this conflict provided the costs of ending it do not outweigh the benefits to our side." If countries would yield disputed territory and forget past bloodshed, a war might be avoided. If political parties gave up their agendas and commitments, they need never reach an impasse. School strikes could be avoided if teachers would uncomplainingly accept lowered salaries and increased class sizes. But wise negotiators understand that every unresisted encroachment on the prerogatives of a group invites additional incursions. Moreover, prolonging, even provoking, conflict may serve vital interests.

THE FIVE PAYOFFS OF CONTROVERSY

For many, conflict is an indication that something is wrong. "People should be able to get along better than that!" we say, or "There must be a middle ground somewhere!" A lot can be gained from ending conflicts. But there are important payoffs for one or both sides in starting or keeping a fight going. These payoffs are *connection, definition, revitalization, reconnaissance,* and *replication.* Let's briefly look at each.

Connection

Conflict is a form of exchange, communication, even negotiation. Nine-year-old boys, teachers complain, seldom interact with girls of the same age except when they quarrel or fight. But this "fighting" and "rivalry" are commonly the awkward beginnings of heterosexuality. This example illustrates that among groups, whatever else they accomplish, disputes establish and maintain relationships. This function of conflict is called **connection**.

Connection works similarly *within groups.* Couples whom everyone describes as "not getting along" are doing just that, but in a way that can be socially objectionable. In domestic disputes, for instance, husbands and wives are making connections even though they attract the police in the process. Troublesome, yes, but a connection, nonetheless. Few have to argue or fight. They can just walk away. But what they lose if they walk are things they value. In the case of an abused spouse, for instance, it might be the income supporting herself and her children. Walking away also means losing a way of "negotiating" one's relationship with the other person. It may be a distorted, unfortunate, perhaps even deadly form of negotiation, but it is the only way that some people know.

Within groups conflict can also work to release tensions that might otherwise harm the group. When people on the same side squabble, it may, in the long run, help keep the group together, keep connection.

Definition

Another function of conflict is definition. **Definition** is the process by which rank and membership are established. Conflict *among groups* heightens the sense of "us" versus "them." "If you aren't with us, you're agin us," the old saying goes. Conflict sharpens exterior boundaries and defines who is on "our" side and who is on "theirs." This is particularly valuable to power holders. They need to know who is "reliable."

The point of this for conflict analysis is to emphasize the value of picking fights and keeping them going. Regardless of the issue in question, this underlying dynamic pertains and helps keep the group's essential nature clear and separate from that of all other groups.

Conflict within groups focuses and accentuates the differences between ranks and social levels. The boss demonstrates his rank and authority in the process of telling employees what to do. The union leader proves her rank and authority by successfully resisting the boss.

Revitalization

Another function of conflict is **revitalization,** a process in which group values are reinvigorated. Conflict *among groups* revitalizes traditions, norms, and values. When Saddam Hussein picked a fight with the United States of America, promising the "mother of all battles," his holy war distracted many Iraqis from the costs imposed on them by Saddam's misrule and, instead, focused his people on the values that Iraqis share in common. The moral of this story is that power holders, particularly those who need to nourish their power, may benefit from conflict.

Even ritualized conflict revitalizes traditions, norms, and values. Varsity college football or basketball provides an example. The "Fighting Irish," the Georgetown "Hoyas," and the "Spartans" of U.S.C. all engage in ritualized conflict with competing schools, and, in doing so, revitalize school spirit and values.

Like varsity athletics, public controversies are controlled conflict; like varsity athletics, such disputes reinvigorate group traditions, norms, and values. Sometimes this is a fringe benefit of the controversy, but sometimes it is employed as a prime function.

Within groups conflict encourages, even requires, individuals to recommit themselves to group values. This is why harassment and hazing form part of the initiation ritual in so many groups. Hazing may drive some away, but those who remain are the more tightly bonded for it. The "beating in" practiced by street gangs is a dramatic example. To demonstrate their "heart," kids wanting to be members voluntarily take a severe beating from the gang. During the beating initiates are expected to fight back, showing they have courage, while simultaneously demanding, "More love!" The "love" in question is an even fiercer beating. Asking for even more punishment proves the initiate's commitment and loyalty to the values of the gang. Gang members, in their turn, prove their commitment to the gang's rites of initiation, however unpleasant they may be.

Reconnaissance

Information gathering is called **reconnaissance**. Small-scale conflicts help gauge whether large-scale conflicts are winnable. New teachers face "testing" by their students to see how serious the teachers are about school rules and procedures and what they are prepared to do to enforce them. Students deliberately break small rules to see how safe it would be to break bigger ones. Similarly, new prison inmates are challenged by experienced "yard birds" to find out how tough they are and to learn whether they can be preyed upon at acceptable cost. Likewise, those disputing such issues as animal rights, capital punishment, abortion, or what have you, are in effect sending out reconnaissance patrols that feel out the enemies' strength. *Among groups* conflict serves this information-gathering purpose.

Within groups internal conflict provides power holders information about the strength of those challenging their leadership. The challengers gather similar intelligence. In other words, internal skirmishes test the will and the resources of the leadership and their opposition. Party mavericks will often promote dark-horse challengers against established candidates to see just how strong the party favorites are.

Replication

The process by which adversaries come to act like each other is called **replication.** Replication's most important function is *within the group.* During a struggle, persons within conflicted groups tend to replicate one another in behavior and, sometimes, even in manner of dress. Imagine a college Homecoming Day football game. Students, staff, and alumni wear school colors, sing the school's fight song, and generally celebrate a common tradition and common values. Similarly, the military promotes rivalry and ritualized conflict among different units or branches of the service. In this way common values are strengthened and group pressure is brought to bear on individuals to perform up to the level of the group.

Among groups adversaries commonly replicate each other's tactics and structure, even when their philosophies are miles apart. Perhaps the most compelling example is provided by the cold war that followed World War II. As this struggle progressed, the tactics of the United States more and more closely resembled that of the Soviets'. To respond to Soviet initiatives, the United States engaged in counterterrorism, sponsored front groups, developed disinformation (false information) campaigns, spied on its own citizens, and sponsored covert operations against freely elected governments. This paradox of a free nation increasingly aping a tyrannical one did not go unnoticed. For example, it provided the material for many of the espionage novels of the period.

The following figure shows how the functions of conflict parallel each other among groups and within groups.

The Functions of Conflict
(Adapted from Coser)

Function	Among groups	Within groups
1. Connection	Serves communication, negotiation, and release of tension	Serves communication, negotiation, and release of tension
2. Definition	Sharpens exterior boundaries	Sharpens internal boundaries
3. Revitalization	Revitalizes mores and traditions	Strengthens underlying values of membership
4. Reconnaissance	Gets information for peacemaking or war	Power holders probe strength of challengers and vice versa
5. Replication	Given a balance of power, generates similarity of structure	Generates a similarity of behavior

Now that we have reviewed the functions of conflict, here are specific steps for using them to analyze disputes.

STEP 1
Ask of any dispute, could the argument be serving any of the functions of conflict?

Keep in mind that the point of the struggle may not really be the issue in dispute. The conflict may have more to do with strengthening group values, finding out who is loyal or disloyal, revitalizing values, getting reconnaissance data, and so forth. Allow for this possibility while weighing the argument.

STEP 2
Ask who, specifically, might benefit from maintaining the dispute?

Everybody in a group may not get the same benefits or pay the same costs. Who does the sweating and who gets the glory? What do they pay and what do they get for it? (Also see chapter 17.)

STEP 3

Consider what might happen to the group if the dispute were actually settled.

Would members of the group no longer feel there was a point to belonging? Would they quit paying dues, making contributions, or donating their labor? Would they continue to hold the leadership in special regard? Would they each go looking for other causes?

LIMITATIONS

OF THIS APPROACH   It is difficult to discern from text alone whether a controversy has been generated or prolonged for ulterior motives. Discerning people's intentions is, at best, problematic, but it's still important.

It should be noted that resisting oppression or undoing injustice may well require conflict. As Frederick Douglass pointed out, "If there is no struggle there is no progress. . . . Power concedes nothing without a demand. It never did and it never will."

CHAPTER HIGHLIGHTS

Provoking or maintaining controversy pays off in many ways. This chapter explains how controversy serves

- connection,
- definition,
- revitalization,
- reconnaissance, and
- replication.

It also lays out steps for employing this knowledge in a search for hidden agendas.

Related Chapters in This Text

4 Definitions
6 Name-Calling
7 Presuppositions
9 Authority
14 Responsibility
17 The Nature of Society

T E S T   Y O U R S E L F

Here is an imagined conflict. The League for the Liberation of Laboratory Animals is picketing selected research laboratories around the nation. Attracted when pickets who, through civil disobedience, attempt to shut down the laboratories, the media is getting sensational footage of police arresting grandmotherly women for refusing to obey cease-and-desist orders. Protesters display gruesome photo enlargements of animals alleged to have been maimed in useless experiments. Sound bites feature earnest protesters recanting horrific tales of experiments on the eyes of helpless rabbits to ensure the safety of eye makeup, mascara, and other cosmetics.

The situation becomes more volatile when a spokesperson for Scientists' Alliance for Ethical Experimentation on Animals arrives at a key demonstration site to denounce the League for the Liberation of Laboratory Animals. She claims that their photo enlargements are fakes and that their sound bites are falsehoods. Jeering Liberationists surround the spokesperson, and police are required to extricate her from the agitated crowd.

Indicate which of the following outcome descriptions are in accord with the functions of conflict.

Outcome Descriptions	In Accord	Not in Accord
1. The League for the Liberation of Laboratory Animals gains greater knowledge of the limits of police tolerance.		
2. As the civil disobedience escalates, members of the Scientists' Alliance for Ethical Experimentation on Animals react with increasing resignation.		
3. Members of the League for the Liberation of Laboratory Animals develop a better sense of what they can achieve by negotiating with the Scientists' Alliance for Ethical Experimentation.		
4. The leadership of the Scientists' Alliance for Ethical Experimentation gets a better sense of who among their members can be counted on in a pinch.		
5. League for the Liberation of Laboratory Animals membership renewals increase and financial contributions also gain substantially.		
6. The recently shaky leadership position of the president of the League for the Liberation of Laboratory Animals becomes more solid. Meanwhile a rival's agitation for a change in leadership becomes muted.		

Outcome Descriptions	In Accord	Not in Accord
7. A significant number of members of the League for the Liberation of Laboratory Animals drop out after being pressured to commit themselves to the organization's increasingly militant course of action. Many of those remaining say, "Good riddance!"		
8. The Scientists' Alliance for Ethical Experimentation begins conducting press conferences and making press releases. Some members even advocate counterdemonstrations.		
9. A number of members of the League for the Liberation of Laboratory Animals, who initially opposed civil disobedience, "make the jump" and support the more militant tactic.		
10. Members of the Scientists' Alliance for Ethical Experimentation gain in mutual conviction that the elimination of animal experimentation will largely destroy meaningful research in America.		

AFTERWORD

America grows more diverse daily, and as this pluralism increases, disagreement accelerates. As these quarrels multiply, advocates of every type clamor more shrilly for your support. Having put this book to use, you know better how and when to respond. With your command of a new set of tools, you now have the means to ask penetrating questions and to evaluate the answers systematically. Without such a procedure, you might as well be pitchforking water.

The point of evaluating disagreements critically is to make thoughtful choices rather than simply to fall into a conflict. Looking for points of reconciliation in an orderly way also enables you to better determine which controversies can be settled and which cannot.

There is, of course, far more to analyzing controversy than this text covers, but you have to begin somewhere. That is what this adaptable tool box of techniques provides—a powerful beginning that emphasizes the following:

- Problems of understanding

  ✔ how slogans serve persuasion
  ✔ how reifications cloak urgent issues
  ✔ how definitions aid persuasion
  ✔ how pseudo solutions displace real solutions
  ✔ how name-calling obscures legitimate concerns

- Problems of fact

  ✔ how one disputant's fact can be another's foolishness
  ✔ how facts relate to feelings
  ✔ how "facts" depend on consensus and authority
  ✔ the foundation of decision making
  ✔ the function of inquiry blockers

- Problems of value

  ✔ how facts differ from, yet are influenced by, values
  ✔ how values figure into costs and benefits
  ✔ how values relate to assigning credit or blame

- Meta problems

  ✔ how logical errors influence disputes
  ✔ the nature and importance of consensus
  ✔ crucial assumptions about the nature of society
  ✔ hidden agendas that perpetuate controversies

155

Now that you are experienced in using this material, where can you turn for further empowerment? Start in this book, especially if you are not yet up to speed in using a modern library. The appendix, *Basic Library Research*, gets you going. Then, for still more finesse in analyzing controversy, you should turn to individual academic disciplines, such as philosophy, the social sciences, religion, history, and so forth. Each academic specialty offers unique insights that are otherwise unavailable to you. Some of the seminal works of these various fields, which influenced the writing of this text, can be found in *Sources and Influences*. These important writings provide insight for deeper understanding.

CHECKLIST

It's often hard to keep track of the many elements involved in analyzing a controversy. You can use the checklist below to keep track of your progress or to see if you've overlooked anything you might want to investigate.

To See If the Controversy You Are Dealing with Is Genuine, Use:

❑ Analyzing Controversy—Chapter 1

To Check for Problems of Understanding, Explore These Issues:

❑ Definitions—Chapter 4
❑ Name-Calling—Chapter 6
❑ Presuppositions—Chapter 7
❑ Pseudo Solutions—Chapter 5
❑ Reification—Chapter 3
❑ Slogans—Chapter 2

To See How Facts Relate to Your Controversy, Check Out the Following:

❑ Appendix: Basic Library Research
❑ Authority—Chapter 9
❑ Feelings, Facts, and Logic—Chapter 8
❑ Inquiry Blockers—Chapter 11
❑ Operationalizing—Chapter 10

To Investigate How Problems of Value Are Involved, Look Into:

❑ Benefits and Costs—Chapter 13
❑ Fact and Value—Chapter 12
❑ Responsibility—Chapter 14

To Look for Other Possible Problems, See:

❑ The Nature of Consensus—Chapter 16
❑ The Nature of Society—Chapter 17
❑ What's Illogical?—Chapter 15
❑ Why Controversies Persist—Chapter 18

Glossary

Absolute benefit (cost) Something valued (or disvalued) intrinsically, that is, in and for itself. **107**

Ad hominem An attack on the presenter of an argument, generally intended to distract from the argument. **44**

Argument A structure of thought, usually proceeding from premises to conclusion. **126**

Benefit(s) What someone judges to be of value. **103**

Community A body of individuals considered a unity for some reason. **95**

Community of judgment People who share common ways of reasoning and values. **96**

Conclusion In logic, a proposition determined from the premises of an argument. **125**

Conflict model A theory that holds that society is a loose amalgamation of groups struggling for contradictory goals and limited resources. **141**

Connection (in conflict) Interaction between individuals or groups. **148**

Consensus Agreement. **130**

Consensus model A theory of society that assumes common agreements and purposes among its members. **139**

Costs What someone judges to be of negative value. **103**

Criteria of judgment Characteristics affecting judgment of what something is and how to deal with it. The basis of classification. **35, 74**

Definition (in conflict) Specification of group membership and rank. **148**

Delegitimate (delegitimize, delegitimization) To speak about or treat something as of little value, or insignificant. **44**

Dissensus Lack of agreement. **16**

Divisible benefit (cost) Benefits (or costs) that can be had by some and not by others. **104**

Evaluative statements Statements containing judgmental phrases. **55**

Evidential usage What a community uses to "prove" an argument or point. **95**

Explicit assumption Stated premise to an argument. **116**

Explicit definition A definition that is expressed without ambiguity. **30**

Expressive disputes Disputes created to attract attention, as in an advertising campaign, or one that vents the antagonisms of a traditional rivalry; for example, "debates" between Republicans and Democrats. **6**

Generalization A statement that is broadly applicable. **21**

Hypothesis A provisional explanation. **80**

Implicit definition A distinction people actually make in practice but don't acknowledge in so many words. **29**

Implied assumption Unstated premise to an argument. **116**

Individualistic model A theory of society that stresses the importance of individual differences and asserts that all social groups are nothing more than a composition of individuals. **142**

Indivisible benefit (cost) Benefits (or costs) which must be shared by all. **104**

Inquiry blockers Answers or responses that brings questioning to a close, usually prematurely. **86**

Interests The concerns or priorities of individuals. **46**

Interpretative authority The authority to explain a source authority, usually individuals in special roles with specific credentials. **72**

Invalid argument An argument in which the conclusion does not follow from the premises. **126**

Lemmas Preliminary conclusions. **62**

Loaded words Emotionally charged words. **125**

Logic A system of organizing thought, particularly with the goal of generating new ideas from previous information. **124**

Motto A short expression, word, phrase, or statement of a guiding principle. **14**

Name-calling Using disparaging words to describe someone, often with the intent of making that person, or his or her concerns, appear to be of little value. **44**

Nonevaluative statements The statement that remains when conditions of judgment have been removed. These are either perception statements, reports, or deductions. **55**

Operationalizing A procedure for reducing vagueness and assisting evaluation or measurement. **79**

Perception statement A statement about what one sees, hears, feels, tastes, or smells. **55**

Personification Treating as a person something that is not. **23**

Positional benefit (cost) Something valued (or disvalued) extrinsically, that is, as a means to other ends. **107**

Positivistic (from Positivism) Believing that only what is directly observable can be a basis of knowledge. **68**

Pragmatic Focused on practical results. **81**

Premise A statement used to construct an argument. **125**

Presuppositions Deep assumptions, often made by both parties to an argument. **52**

Pseudo solution A suggestion that sounds like it can solve a problem, but is practically useless. **38**

Reconnaissance (in conflict) Information gathering. **150**

Reify (reification) To treat an abstraction or a vague general term as though it were a concrete, even living, thing; e.g. "Nature is saddened by water pollution." **22**

Relativistic Lacking commitment to a particular standard. **97**

Replication (in conflict) Development of parallel structure to a competitor. **150**

Report statements Statements indicating second-hand information. **56**

Revitalization (in conflict) Renewing of group values. **149**

Rule of reciprocation The disposition to give something in return. **65**

Slogan A vague word, phrase, or statement, often used to inspire agreement; often in the form of mottoes. Slogans mask over potential conflicts. **13**

Source authority Documents, institutions, or individuals that people turn to for fundamental guidance. **72**

Substantial benefit (cost) A benefit (cost) recognized as such across a variety of groups. **109**

Syllogism An argument with two premises and a conclusion. **125**

Symbolic benefit (cost) A benefit (cost) recognized as such within restricted groups. **109**

Theorem A conclusion judged to have broad importance, usually only in a formal system. **125**

Undistributed middle A syllogism where both premises have the same predicate. **126**

Unsound argument An argument with at least one factually false premise. **126**

Answers to Test Yourself

Chapter 2

Slogan	Acceptable versus Unacceptable Interpretations
"Support quality education."	*Acceptable:* 1. Pass the school tax increase. *Acceptable:* 2. Require everyone to take two years of algebra (or a foreign language, or . . .) *Unacceptable:* 1. Let's go shopping. *Unacceptable:* 2. Allow more illiterates to graduate.
"Just say "No" to drugs."	*Acceptable:* 1. Refuse drug dealer's offers. *Acceptable:* 2. Turn in dealers. *Unacceptable:* 1. Snort angel dust. *Unacceptable:* 2. Stand in front of drug store and scream "No!"
"You can't solve school problems by just throwing money at them."	*Acceptable:* 1. We need to change what we are spending for. *Acceptable:* 2. Solving some school problems requires changed attitudes, not more spending. *Unacceptable:* 1. A new $30 million library is the key to improved learning. *Unacceptable:* 2. Raise per student spending by 50 percent.
"Reduce government interference in our lives."	*Acceptable:* 1. Outlaw FBI surveillance of all domestic political groups. *Acceptable:* 2. Replace the federal income tax with a flat tax. *Unacceptable:* 1. Authorize the CIA to make domestic wiretaps. *Unacceptable:* 2. Increase penalties for homosexual acts between consenting adults.

Chapter 3

The odd-numbered statements contain reifications; the even ones do not.

In number 1 both "foreign trade" and "America" are reifications. Trade in autos is not the same thing as trade in rice. Different Americans are affected differently.

In number 2, "Atlanta Braves" is a group concept because the team's being on a losing streak does not tell us about individual performance. A pitcher might have the most wins ever, and yet the team may still be on a losing streak.

In number 3, both Germany and Central Europe are reifications. We are probably talking about heads of government, not arbitrary individuals in any given country.

In number 4, Beethoven's Fifth Symphony can only be played by an orchestra. Individual players can only participate by playing specific parts.

In number 5, generation X is a reification. It at best indicates an average. Individual members of the generation can still be quite ambitious.

Chapter 4

Term	Explicit Definition	(Possible) Implicit Definition
criminal	(a person) guilty of a crime (*Webster's Encyclopedic Unabridged Dictionary*)	a person rumored to be engaged in improper activities
fascist	a member of the Fascisti, an Italian right-wing political movement	anyone displaying authority
murder	the unlawful killing of another human being with malice aforethought	any killing I don't approve of
obscene	offensive to modesty or decency; indecent, lewd	a display of nudity

Chapter 5

The proposed solutions to items 2, 3, 5, 8, 9, and 10 all could fail. Items 1, 4, 6, and 7 are pseudo solutions.

Chapter 6

A.

List 1: Words That Recognize Interest	List 2: Words That Reject Interest
spontaneous	immature
playful	cold-blooded
frank	aggressive
focused	overstriving
calm	sneaky
bored	wild
self-controlled	unmannered
assertive	stubborn
persistent	rude

B.

1. Sam is <u>wild</u>. He is <u>playful</u> when he shouldn't be.
2. Sam is <u>cold-blooded</u>. He is <u>calm</u> when he shouldn't be.
3. Sam is <u>aggressive</u>. He is <u>assertive</u> when he shouldn't be.
4. Sam is <u>overstriving</u>. He is <u>persistent</u> when he shouldn't be.
5. Sam is <u>rude</u>. He is <u>frank</u> when he shouldn't be.

Chapter 7

False Statement	Presupposition
1. Mary was seen stealing Jack's pen.	(a) The person seeing the situation (in good light) had his glasses on. (b) What someone saw her take was a pen. (c) She intended to keep it. (d) The pen belonged to Jack.
2. Jack wrote that he could see his long-dead uncle standing right in front of him.	(a) Jack's uncle is actually dead. (b) The letter is actually from Jack. (c) Jack's eyesight is good.
3. The *Sacramento Bee* reported that Sam embezzled funds.	(a) The report is accurate. (b) The identity of the embezzler is correct. (c) The money was not just borrowed.
4. Sam says he can feel his foot is frostbitten.	(a) We heard him correctly. (b) His foot is not merely asleep. (c) It's not referred pain.
5. Experts claim that Coca-Cola improves cerebral functioning.	(a) The claimants are not really experts. (b) The experts drank too many Coca-Colas before reaching the conclusion.

Chapter 8

The democracy(+) which embodies and guarantees our freedom(+) is not powerless(-), passive(-) or blind(-), nor is it in retreat(-). It has no intention of giving way to the savage fantasies(-) of its adversaries. It is not prepared to give advance blessing to its own destruction(-)."

–Pierre Elliott Trudeau

Everything ponderous(-), vicious(-), and solemnly clumsy(-), all long-winded(-) and boring(-) types of style are developed in profuse variety among Germans.
                                                                    –Friedrich Nietzche

For what are the triumphs(-) of war planned by ambition(-), executed by violence(-), and consummated by devastation(-)? The means are the sacrifice(+) of many, the end the bloated aggrandizement(-) of the few."
                                                                    –Charles Colton

With all their faults, trade-unions have done more for humanity than any other organization of men that ever existed. They have done more for decency(+), for honesty(+), for education(+), for the betterment(+) of the race, for the development of character(+) in man, than any other association of men."
                                                                    –Clarence Darrow

It is the American vice(-), the democratic disease(-) which expresses its tyranny(-) by reducing everything unique to the level of the herd(-).
                                                                    –Henry Miller

Chapter 9

Example:	Sketch of Answer
Harry kills Sam. To what extent is Harry responsible for his act?	The criteria for "being responsible" are likely to be at issue here. Intention, sobriety, avoidability, awareness are some criteria for examining Harry's action. Possibly lawyers, psychiatrists, clergy, and Harry himself will be brought into the dispute.
1. The Argus company is contributing an unacceptable level of waste runoff into the Mississippi river. What criteria of acceptability is relevant here? Who decides? Does anyone dispute this?	Is Argus really the source and is the Mississippi the recipient of pollution? What is the "legal limit"? Engineers, lawyers, and judges are some of the authorities likely to be appealed to here.
2. Art, but not pornography, should be admitted to publicly funded museums. Who decides what is pornography? Why they? Does anyone else cite a different authority here?	"Pornography" is notoriously difficult to define. What is pornographic as far as children are concerned is often acceptable for adults. Pictures of genitalia in one context, e.g., medical books, may be acceptable. In other contexts, they may not be. On this issue, no one is widely recognized as an expert, although legal and clerical authorities are likely to claim jurisdiction here.
3. American industry is not competitive with Japanese industry. What standards are relevant to establish competitiveness? Who sets the standards? Is there a dispute about this?	Which specific industries are being compared? Is nationality determined by ownership or location? Economists and politicians might claim authority here.
4. The national monetary inflation level is undesirable. How is this determined? Who determines it? Does everyone agree on this authority?	Is the inflation level accurately measured? Are there alternative measures? What is an acceptable level? Economists, politicians, and businesspersons will probably claim expertise here.

Example:	Sketch of Answer
5. Only religious organizations should be exempted from federal taxes. What counts as a religious organization? Who says so? Are there any disagreements about who can say so?	What counts as a "religious organization"? Must it be an established organization, or does a storefront church count? Legal and religious authorities will likely be involved in this dispute, particularly the IRS.

Chapter 10

Attempted Operationalization of the Hypothesis: Gender differences are rooted in the brain.
Comments

1. Brains develop differently in male and female fetuses.
   A different developmental sequence may not finally result in what we consider gender difference. This statement is not a good operationalization; nor does it count against the hypothesis.
2. Brain differences between men and women help explain differences in occupation.
   This could be an operationalization. It does not count against the hypothesis.
3. Females will not generally become engineers.
   This does not mention anything about the brain being involved. Nor does it count against the hypothesis.
4. Boys can throw better than girls.
   This is neither an operationalization nor counterevidence to the hypothesis.
5. The wearing of high heels is determined by amygdalic functioning.
   This is a possible operationalization.

Chapter 11

Reformulate the inquiry-blocking statements given below as questions that pursue further inquiry, e.g.,

"It is clear he doesn't know what he is talking about" becomes
"Does he know what he is talking about?"

Inquiry Blockers
Comments

1. It's natural for him to expect more than he deserves. Does he expect more than he deserves?
2. Not you, nor I, nor anyone knows why oats, peas, beans, or barley grow. How do oats, peas, beans or barley grow?
3. I just know he's a murderer! Is he a murderer?
4. A little bird told me that she's in love with him. Is she in love with him?
5. Sure, Joe's selfish; that's just human nature. Why is Joe so selfish?

Chapter 12

We would accept none of the statements as disproving that beheading is fatal to humans. Reports of peoples' beliefs or attitudes toward a fact, i.e., beheading is fatal, do not disprove the fact.

Chapter 13

Answers: (Expressed here only as which side of the continuum the benefit, or cost, is on. Where they are located on the continuum is subject to interpretation.)
2. Divisible, Absolute, Symbolic
3. Divisible, Absolute, Substantial

4. Indivisible? (depends on what you value), Absolute, Symbolic? (Saving this species could also have substantial value, not just for whaling, but long-term value in terms of scientific knowledge.)
5. Divisible, Absolute, Substantial
6. Divisible, Absolute, Substantial (How you get it does not seem to change the cost typology.)
7. Indivisible, Absolute, Substantial (A damaged ozone layer costs money.)
8. Divisible, Positional, Symbolic

Chapter 14

1. With regard to Harrington's statement, the impoverished person has diminished responsibility. The area circled should be on the right side of the continuum.
2. With regard to Johnson's statement, the issue of responsibility is obscured by another question. How responsible are the ignorant for their own condition? Where the circle goes depends on that answer.
3. With respect to Phaedrus's statement, the term "master" suggests someone else is primarily responsible. The circle goes on the "not responsible" end of the continuum.
4. Jerome's statement is difficult to place. Presumably, if it is a "blunder" to be poor, the circle should go somewhere on the "responsible" side.
5. This Yiddish proverb wryly suggests that the individual is sufficiently responsible to make poverty "no honor," but not sufficiently responsible to make it a "disgrace." Perhaps the middle of the continuum should be circled. It's a tough call.

Chapter 15

1. Sally is studying calculus. She must want to be an engineer. Engineers use calculus all the time.
   Rearranged as a syllogism, this looks like:
   > Engineers use calculus all the time.
   > Sally is studying calculus.
   > Sally must want to be an engineer.

   This is much more subtle than a simple analysis of syllogisms can handle. There is a hidden premise that enables the conclusion, that is, whoever studies what engineers use must want to be an engineer. This hidden premise is generally false. So the argument is at least unsound. In addition, the use of calculus is not unique to engineers. Merely studying calculus does not mean Sally wants to be an engineer, even if we were to accept the hidden premise as hypothetically true. We might dodge the issue of what Sally wants to be by changing the premises so that we get the related syllogism:
   > Engineers study calculus.
   > Sally studies calculus.
   > So Sally must be an engineer.

   This related train of thought suffers from the fallacy of the undistributed middle.
2. Jack must be a conservative, since he reads the very conservative *National Review* regularly.
   To construct a syllogism we need to supply a hidden premise (asterisked below).
   > *All regular readers of the *National Review* are conservatives.
   > Jack reads the very conservative *National Review* regularly.
   > Jack must be a conservative.

   This valid argument is not sound unless the added premise is true. That premise may be highly likely so that Jack is very likely a conservative. But this kind of probabilistic thinking goes beyond what syllogisms can handle. (This is an encouragement to further study.)
3. My brother's goat gives milk. Your goat must give milk, too.

This requires a premise to the effect that all goats are alike in what they provide us as nourishment. The argument in syllogistic form might look like this:

> *All goats give us the same kinds of nourishment.
> My brother's goat gives milk (which provides humans nourishment).
> Your goat must give milk, too.

A valid, though possibly unsound, argument, because the added premise is probably false.

4. All Chinese are communists. Fred is a communist, so he must be Chinese.
   As a syllogism this looks like:

> All Chinese are communists.
> Fred is a communist.
> Fred must be Chinese.

The fallacy of the undistributed middle. The syllogism is invalid, even apart from the likely false premise that all Chinese are communists.

5. Real men don't eat quiche. Sally is not a real man. So Sally eats quiche.
   The syllogistic form looks like:

> Real men don't eat quiche.
> Sally is not a real man.
> So Sally eats quiche.

Even apart from the pun on "real"—such punning confounds simple logic because it depends on multiple meanings—this argument is invalid. It negates the antecedent.

Chapter 16

All "answers" are necessarily guesstimates. More information would be needed for more refined judgments.

1. State vouchers should be issued to help parents who want to opt for private schooling.
   Pro: Enterprisers, Moralists, Disaffecteds, Seculars
   Con: Upbeats, 60's Democrats, New Dealers, Passive Poor
2. Drug usage should be decriminalized.
   Pro: 60's Democrats, Partisan Poor, Followers
   Con: Enterprisers, Moralists, New Dealers, Passive Poor

Chapter 17

Case Example	Individualistic	Conflict	Consensus
2. "American schools had to maintain . . .	No, because of the reification	Yes, conflict emphasized	No, conflict emphasized
3. "Human life in common is . . .	No, indicates individuality negative	No, antagonisms not even hinted	Yes, stresses need for agreement
4. "Society looks to higher . . .	No, utilizes reification	No, no hint of conflict	Yes, reifies "society"
5. "Ein Volk; Ein Reich . . .	Definitely not; "Volk" and "Reich" are reifications	No, no conflict between three components	Yes, society is unity of people, empire, and leader

Chapter 18

All of the outcomes are in accord with the functions of conflict.

SOURCES AND INFLUENCES

The sources given below contain works that the authors found provide impetus to their own inquiries into the topics of each chapter. They are also works that the authors have used in their classes as basic reading. The readings are interesting and accessible to the technically unpracticed student. They are by no means intended to represent the most up-to-date or technically sophisticated literature available on the topics.

CHAPTER 1: ANALYZING CONTROVERSY: AN OVERVIEW

Dewey, John. 1933. *How We Think*. Boston: D. C. Heath.

People, Press and Politics, The. 1987. Washington, DC: Times-Mirror.

Pierce, Charles Sanders. 1955. "How to Make Our Ideas Clear." In *The Age of Analysis*, ed. Morton G. White. New York: Mentor.

Weimer, David L., and Aidan R. Vining. 1992. *Policy Analysis: Concepts and Practice*. 2nd ed. Englewood Cliffs, NJ: Prentice Hall.

CHAPTER 2: SLOGANS

Komisar, B. Paul. 1971. "The Language of Education." In *The Encyclopedia of Education*. Vol. 5, ed. L. C. Leighton. New York: Macmillan.

Komisar, B. Paul, and James E. McClellan, 1961. "The Logic of Slogans." In *Language and Concepts in Education*, ed. B. Othaniel Smith and Robert H. Ennis. Chicago: Rand McNally.

Ryle, Gilbert. 1965. "Systematically Misleading Expressions." In *Logic and Language*, ed. Anthony Flew. Garden City: Doubleday Anchor.

Walton, Mary. 1986. *The Deming Management Method*. New York: Putnam.

CHAPTER 3: REIFICATION

Lindblom, Charles E. 1959 (Spring). "The Science of 'Muddling Through.'" *Public Administration Review* 19:79–88.

Pfeffer, Jeffrey. 1982. *Organizations and Organization Theory*. Boston: Pitman.

Perrow, Charles. 1979. *Complex Organizations*. Oakland, NJ: Scott-Foresman.

CHAPTER 4: DEFINITIONS

Austin, J. L. 1963. "The Meaning of a Word." In *Philosophy and Ordinary Language*, ed. Charles E. Caton. Urbana: University of Illinois Press.

Hart, H. L. A. 1965. "The Ascription of Responsibility and Rights." In *Logic and Language*, ed. Anthony Flew. Garden City: Doubleday Anchor.

Schleffler, Israel. 1960. *The Language of Education.* Springfield, IL: Charles C. Thomas.

Wilson, John. 1989. *Thinking with Concepts.* New York: Cambridge.

Wittgenstein, Ludwig. 1967. *Philosophische Untersuchungen.* Frankfurt-am-Main: Suhrkamp.

CHAPTER 5: PSEUDO SOLUTIONS

Janis, Irving L. 1989. *Crucial Decisions: Leadership in Policymaking and Crisis Management.* New York: Free Press.

Kliebard, Herbert M. 1975. "The Rise of the Scientific Curriculum and Its Aftermath." *Curriculum Theory Network* 5:1.

Langer, Ellen J. 1982. "The Illusion of Control." In *Judgment Under Uncertainty: Heuristics and Biases,* ed. Daniel Kahneman, Paul Slovic, and Amos Tversky. Cambridge: Cambridge University Press.

CHAPTER 6: NAME-CALLING

Campbell, Bernard. 1970. *The Roots of Language: Biological and Social Factors in Psycholinguistics,* ed. John Morton. Urbana, IL: University of Illinois Press.

Corbett, Edward P. J. 1971. *Classical Rhetoric for the Modern Student.* 2nd ed. New York: Oxford University Press.

Searle, John R. 1960. *Speech Acts.* London: Cambridge University Press.

CHAPTER 7: PRESUPPOSITIONS

Austin, J. L. 1965. *How to Do Things with Words.* New York: Oxford University Press.

Jacobs, Roderick A., and Peter S. Rosenbaum. 1968. *English Transformational Grammar.* Waltham, MA: Blaisdell.

Noll, James W., ed. 1987. *Taking Sides: Clashing Views on Controversial Educational Issues.* Guilford, CT: Dushkin.

CHAPTER 8: FEELINGS, FACTS, AND LOGIC

Black, Max. 1970. *Margins of Precision: Essays in Logic and Language.* Ithaca: Cornell University Press.

Chisholm, Roderick M. 1965. "The Theory of Appearing." In *Perceiving, Sensing, and Knowing,* ed. Robert J. Swartz. Garden City, NY: Anchor.

Cialdini, Robert B. 1984. *Influence: The New Psychology of Modern Persuasion.* New York: Quill.

Maultsby, Maxie, Jr. 1984. *Rational Behavior Therapy.* Englewood Cliffs, NJ: Prentice Hall.

Stevenson, Charles L. 1963. *Facts and Values: Studies in Ethical Analysis.* New Haven: Yale University Press.

CHAPTER 9: CRITERIA AND AUTHORITY

Benn, S. I., and R. S. Peters. 1965. *The Principles of Political Thought: Social Foundations of the Democratic State.* New York: Free Press.

Keegan, John. 1987. *The Mask of Command.* New York: Viking.
March, James J., and Herbert A. Simon. 1958. *Organizations.* New York: Wiley.
Sennett, Richard. 1981. *Authority.* New York: Vintage.

CHAPTER 10: OPERATIONALIZING

Bunge, Mario. 1963. *Causality.* Cleveland: World Publications.
Carnap, Rudolf. 1953. "Testability and Meaning." In *Readings in the Philosophy of Science,* ed. Herbert Feigl and May Brodbeck. New York: Appleton-Century-Crofts.
Schlick, Moritz. 1970. "Meaning and Verification." In *Theory of Meaning,* ed. Adrienne and Keith Lehrer. Englewood Cliffs, NJ: Prentice Hall.
Waismann, Friedrich. 1965. "Verifiability." In *Logic and Language,* ed. Anthony Flew. Garden City: Doubleday Anchor.

CHAPTER 11: INQUIRY-BLOCKERS

McClellan, James E. 1967. "B. F. Skinner's Philosophy of Human Nature: A Sympathetic Criticism." In *Psychological Concepts in Education,* ed. Paul B. Komisar and C. J. B. Macmillan. Chicago: Rand McNally.

CHAPTER 12: FACT AND VALUE

Bedford, Errol. 1964. "Emotions." In *Essays in Philosophical Psychology,* ed. Donald F. Gustafson. Garden City, NY: Doubleday.
Berger, Peter L., and Thomas Luckmann. 1967. *The Social Construction of Reality.* Garden City: Anchor Books.
Lewis, C. I. 1946. *An Analysis of Knowledge and Valuation.* LaSalle, IL: Open Court.
MacIntyre, Alasdair. 1988. *Whose Justice? Which Rationality?* Notre Dame, IN: University of Notre Dame Press.
Nietzsche, Friedrich. 1955. *Beyond Good and Evil.* Trans. Marianne Cowan. Chicago: Gateway.
Sesonske, Alexander, and Noel Fleming, eds. 1965. *Plato's Meno.* Belmont, CA: Wadsworth.
Urmson, J. O. 1965. "On Grading." In *Logic and Language,* ed. Anthony Flew. Garden City: Doubleday Anchor.

CHAPTER 13: BENEFITS AND COSTS

Collins, Randal. 1979. *The Credential Society.* New York, Academic Press.
Deci, Edward. 1976 (Winter). "The Hidden Cost of Rewards." *Organizational Dynamics* 4(3).
Green, Thomas F. 1980. *Predicting the Behavior of the Educational System.* Syracuse, NY: Syracuse University Press.
Green, Thomas F. 1980 (July/August). "Weighing the Justice of Inequality." *Change* 12:5.
Hirsch, Fred. 1967. *The Social Limits to Growth.* Cambridge: Harvard University Press.

CHAPTER 14: RESPONSIBILITY

Coleman, J. S., et al. 1966. *Equality of Educational Opportunity.* Washington, DC: U.S. Government Printing Office, p. 325.

Fodor, Jerry. 1968. *Psychological Explanation: An Introduction to the Philosophy of Psychology.* New York: Random House.

Jencks, Christopher. 1972. *Inequality: A Reassessment of the Effect of Family and Schooling in America.* New York: Harper.

Rieff, Phillip. 1966. *The Triumph of the Therapeutic: Uses of Faith after Freud.* New York: Harper and Row.

Taylor, Charles. 1985. *Hegel and Modern Society.* New York: Cambridge University Press.

Toulmin, Stephen. 1960. *Reason in Ethics.* London: Cambridge University Press.

CHAPTER 15: WHAT'S ILLOGICAL?

Crawshay-Williams, Rupert. 1957. *Methods and Criteria of Reasoning: An Inquiry into the Structure of Controversy.* London: Routledge and Kegan Paul.

Flew, Anthony, ed. 1965. *Logic and Language.* Garden City: Doubleday Anchor.

Susskind, Lawrence, and Jeffrey Cruikshank. 1987. *Breaking the Impasse: Consensual Approaches to Resolving Public Disputes.* New York: Basic Books.

CHAPTER 16: NATURE OF CONSENSUS

Fisher, Roger, and William Ury. 1987. *Getting to YES: Negotiating Agreement without Giving In.* New York: Penguin.

MacIntyre, Alasdair. 1981. *After Virtue.* Notre Dame, IN: Notre Dame University Press.

Mansbridge, Jane J. 1980. *Beyond Adversary Democracy.* New York: Basic Books.

Pruit, Dean G., and Jeffry Z. Rubin. 1986. *Social Conflict: Escalation, Stalemate, and Settlement.* New York: Random House.

Raiffa, Howard. 1982. *The Art and Science of Negotiation.* Cambridge, MA: Belknap Press.

Weiss, Michael J. 1988. *The Clustering of America.* New York: Harper and Row.

CHAPTER 17: THE NATURE OF SOCIETY

Boudon, Raymond. 1973. *Education, Opportunity, and Social Inequality.* New York: Wiley.

Bowles, Samuel, and Herbert Gintis. 1976. *Schooling in Capitalist America.* New York: Basic Books.

Merton, Robert K. 1976. *Social Theory and Social Structure.* New York: Harcourt.

CHAPTER 18: WHY CONTROVERSIES PERSIST

Boulding, Kenneth E. 1963. *Conflict and Defense: A General Theory.* New York: Harper Torchbooks.

Coser, Lewis. 1956. *The Functions of Social Conflict.* New York: Free Press.

Dunnigan, James F. 1983. *How to Make War.* New York: Quill.

Schelling, Thomas C. 1960. *The Strategy of Conflict.* Cambridge: Harvard University Press.

APPENDIX:
BASIC LIBRARY RESEARCH*

This appendix includes four sections:

- Basic Library Research
- Creating a Search Strategy
- Facts about Periodicals
- Searching Databases

BASIC LIBRARY RESEARCH

What are the facts? That question is central in analyzing most disputes. Here is a "quick and dirty" four-step process for doing library research.

STEP 1
Use dictionaries, encyclopedias, textbooks, and other general works to provide background information on your topic.

These sources may also include bibliographies that will lead you to additional information on your topic. (There are specialized bibliographies listed in the central catalog, and a librarian can help you find those that are relevant.) Here is how to use these general works.

- Choose a topic of interest.
- Determine the purpose of your research (to establish facts, to inform, to persuade, and so forth).
- Select key words that will help you identify relevant information.
- Broaden or narrow your topic to make it more manageable.

---

*This appendix is based on research guides originally developed by Bernetta Robinson Doane, Coordinator of Bibliographic Instruction, and Martha Lyle, Serials Librarian, both of the Connelly Library, La Salle University, Philadelphia, Pennsylvania. We are grateful for their permission to adapt their materials for use in this book.

STEP 2

Use the on-line (or card) catalog to find books on your topic.

STEP 3

Use periodical indexes and databases (print, CD-ROM and on-line) to find articles in journals, magazines, and newspapers that relate to your topic.

Periodical indexes come in a variety of subject areas. Select the index most appropriate for your topic. (For details, see Creating a Search Strategy below.)

STEP 4

Ask a Reference Librarian to help you find specialized sources and other materials that may be helpful.

In larger libraries you can find a Reference Librarian at the Information or Reference Desk.

CREATING A SEARCH STRATEGY

Creating a search strategy involves "mapping out" the key components of a library research topic. Here is the basic process in steps.

STEP 1

Formulate a topic. Selecting a topic is the most important component of a successful search. State your topic in the form of a question, a phrase, or the title of an article or book on the subject.

Sample topic: Can playing the violin cause repetitive stress injury to wrists and arms?

On the line below, write the subject you are looking for. Use the sample topic as a guide.

Topic: _____

STEP 2

Analyze the topic. Scrutinize the topic and identify *keywords* or *phrases.* If necessary, consult specialized dictionaries, encyclopedias, controlled vocabulary lists, and thesauri for more terms.

STEP 3

Divide the keywords or phrases into concepts.

Sample	Your keywords or Phrases
Concept 1: violin	_____
Concept 2: repetitive stress injury	_____
Concept 3: wrists	_____
Concept 4: arms	_____

STEP 4

Set up a search strategy using Boolean operators.

A Boolean operator refers to the logical use of algebraic terms involving two or more values.

Boolean operators are used in computer database searching to connect research concepts.

Boolean operators use only three words: *and, or,* and *not.* Here is how they work.

"AND" narrows the search topic because both concepts must be in each record.

Concept 1 and Concept 2 and Concept 3

If we specify violin *and* repetitive stress injury *and* wrists, the database will give us a list of sources in which all three concepts are mentioned. This is indicated by the crosshatching in the accompanying diagram.

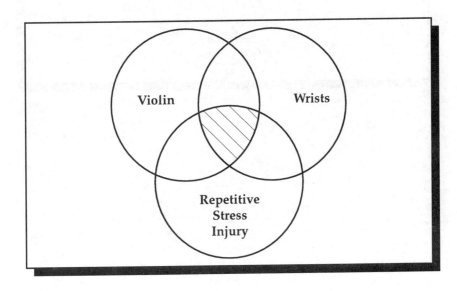

"OR" broadens the search topic because all records containing one or both of the terms are included. If you need to broaden your topic, add synonyms or other phrases to the search strategy.

Concept 1 violins *or* Concept 2 stringed instruments

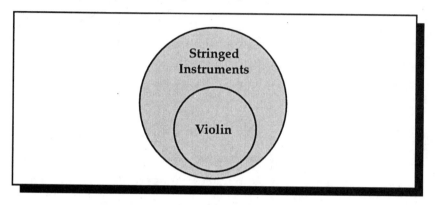

"NOT" eliminates unrelated records containing the concept.

Concept 1 *not* Concept 2 repetitive stress injury *not* carpal tunnel syndrome

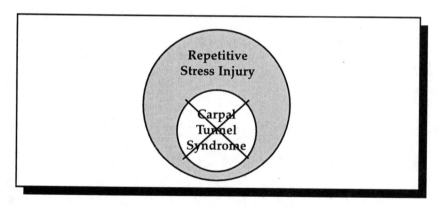

STEP 5

Choose a database.

Choosing the right database is important because publishers construct their indexes (databases) for various subjects. Librarians are trained to help you select the database that best answers your research question. Examples of pertinent databases for the sample topic:

CINAHL	(Nursing)
Expanded Academic Index	(General)
MEDLINE	(Medical)

STEP 6

Execute the search strategy.

This simply means typing the search strategy into the database system. Watch your spelling; most databases look for keywords or phrases in strict alphabetical order.

Because each database service is slightly different, make sure that you read the HELP screens for detailed instructions on how to effectively use the service.

STEP 7

Examine the bibliographic citation/record.

Look at each bibliographic citation/record found. Locate keywords and phrases. See how the concepts of the topic are arranged throughout the record. This will help you to determine which records are actually relevant to the research.

STEP 8

Print.

Print the bibliographic citations related to the research. Remember printing features may vary from one database to the next. Be sure to read the screens.

STEP 9

Check if citations are available in the library.

Now that you have found citations, you need to see if they are available in the library. Use the library's on-line catalog. In many libraries this involves looking at the Main Menu, selecting P for Periodical Title, and typing the full name of the journal, magazine, or newspaper.

FACTS ABOUT PERIODICALS

The term *periodical* is used in libraries to refer to journal, magazine, or newspaper publications. Typically, a university or large college library will have over 1,000 subscriptions to periodicals, covering a wide range of subject areas.

Periodicals are very useful in doing research because:

- they provide the most current information on a subject,
- they help to identify very "new" or "hot" topics of interest that may not be found in books,
- the findings may be limited to a specific concept, and
- older issues may help to provide historical information on the topic.

Periodical Indexes

The most efficient way to locate *articles* on a specific topic is to use a periodical index.

Periodical indexes guide you through the contents of various publications. Some periodical indexes are general in nature and try to cover most subject areas (for example, *Readers' Guide to Periodical Literature* and *Expanded Academic Index*). Others are designed to be more subject-specific (such as *Business Periodicals Index, General Science Index, Psychological Abstracts,* and so on).

Use the index appropriate for your topic. You will find periodical indexes in the print format, CD-ROM, and on-line. CD-ROM and on-line searching are fast ways of retrieving periodical information. Reference librarians are available at the Information Desk for assistance.

Once you have a list of articles on your topics, go to the catalog to determine whether the library owns the periodical publication. At the catalog, type a P for a title search on the name of the periodical.

Scholarly Journal or Popular Magazine

Students frequently want to know whether the periodical in which they have located an article is scholarly or popular (general).

There are no hard-and-fast rules for making a decision because many periodicals have both scholarly and popular elements. Ultimately the student has to become familiar with the publications in a particular subject area and learn to make critical evaluations of each article.

However, listed below are some characteristics that might help you in the selection process.

JOURNAL

- scholarly reader (professor, student, and so forth)

- written by person(s) trained in the subject area

- has a bibliography or references

- specific structure (abstract, methods, conclusion, and so on)

MAGAZINE

- general audience

- written by journalist

- generally no references

- written like a story

SEARCHING DATABASES

Databases are invaluable as timesavers. What used to take many hours of tedious searching can now be done in minutes.

Structure of a Database

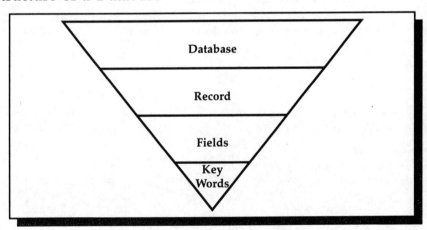

Search Limitations

Here are common limits on a search.

- Subjects covered
- Dates covered
- Frequency of updates
- Currency of information

Selecting a Database

The database you select affects the amount and quality of information retrieved.

- Determine which database best answers your information needs by asking your instructor and/or a librarian.

Access to Database Information

Databases are available in different formats: on-line, CD-ROM, and print. Sometimes the same database is even available in multiple formats. This is important because information that is free for you in one format may not be free in another.

Setting Up a Search Strategy

- Brainstorm: talk with instructors and librarians
- Consult reference sources: dictionaries, encyclopedias, and thesauri
- Develop a list of keywords or phrases
- Connect the keywords or phrases using Boolean operators: *and, or, not*
- Type the search strategy into the database system

Looking at the Search Results

Use what you see on the screen to help you interpret and/or revise your search strategy. Look for:

- Number of hits (records found)
- Are there too many or too few?
- Can you find your keywords or phrases anywhere in the record?

How to Change Search Results

Most databases have help screens and guides to assist you in your searching. Some have common commands, for example:

- Type *help* or *?*
- Function keys (*F1* is generally very helpful)
- Limit the search by using different combinations of Boolean operators

How to Interpret Search Results

- Look at each record for information that is relevant to the topic; for example, keywords, phrases.
- Identify any labels (often abbreviated) used in the record.

Finding the Information in the Library

- Look in the catalog to see if the items retrieved from the search are available in the library.
- To find a periodical article, press P for periodical title and type in the full name of the periodical, that is, *Time, Newsweek,* and so on (this procedure is not standard on all library catalogs; check with librarian).
- To find a book, press T for title or A for author's name.
- If the item is not available in the library, go to the Information Desk and ask about the Interlibrary Loan Service.

Index

Page numbers in **boldface** refer to glossary terms.